COPPERING THE CANNON

by

JAMES CANNON

authorHOUSE™

1663 LIBERTY DRIVE, SUITE 200
BLOOMINGTON, INDIANA 47403
(800) 839-8640
WWW.AUTHORHOUSE.COM

First published by AuthorHouse 12/10/04

ISBN: 1-4208-1034-0 (sc)

Printed in the United States of America
Bloomington, Indiana

This book is printed on acid-free paper.

Table of Contents

Introduction

A good number of books on policing have been published over the years, usually by Chief Constables and other very senior officers. Their books reflect on their careers and society's needs and ills, and offer solutions and possible ways forward. This book is not like that. I was not a very senior officer and I do not want to try to hold forth on society's problems or offer solutions, although I may be unable to resist the odd comment. This is simply the story of an ordinary Policeman, with all the ups and downs that come a Policeman's way, warts and all. I apologise for the language sometimes employed, I am only repeating the language of others. Some of the stories are very gory so beware.

I served in the Larkshire Constabulary for some 18 years, beginning in the early 1970's. High-tec policing was still in the future. There were no computers, mobile phones, or any of the modern paraphernalia of today's Police Service. A good number of police officers were recruited from the armed forces and had seen war service, old style coppers, with a mind-set to match. Many of them still wore the old detachable collars with studs, which I just about remembered were used by my grandfather and father when I was a small boy. The breath test and the Theft Act were just finding their feet. Some laws in regular use went back to the Napoleonic era and we even used one from 1361! Police officers on the beat were still the norm, the select few did have cars, we did have radios, and sometimes they even worked! A whistle for communication was still part of every officer's equipment and truncheons were our main weapon, made of wood and with very limited stopping power. There was no body armour, and helmets were made of covered cork and provided hardly any protection. In any event, they always came off if running or involved in any sort of physical exertion.

The concept of discipline was firmly rooted in military tradition, with ranks based on army structure, even though they were called by other names. There was an officer elite, beginning with the rank of Inspector and continuing up to Chief Constable, with 'other ranks' consisting of Constables and Sergeants. Officers had their own 'Senior Officers Dining Room' at Headquarters and in some Stations, in addition some Stations were provided with a senior officer's loo - no hob-nobbing with other ranks. Police Officers were no longer civilians; they had crossed over to a vocation expecting 30 years of commitment. Resignations were very rare indeed, especially after the first two years of service, although a months notice was all that was required. Constables and Sergeants had to retire at 55, while senior ranks could stay on until they were 60. Retiring officers had little trouble in finding a civilian post within the Police if they so desired, unless they were particularly inept.

Recruitment was very different to the modern practice, with interviews short and unstructured. Instead of senior officers conducting the interviews, it was usually just a Sergeant. The pay was nothing to be excited about; when I joined, my income dropped by more than 20%, or approximately £300 pa less than my previous salary. Recruitment tended to go up and down with the prevailing employment situation in the economy. When unemployment was high, more people wanted to join. When unemployment was low so was the intake of recruits, there were much better paid jobs out there. The Constabulary was known as a Police Force, rather than a Police Service. In short it was very different to the policing we know today especially in management and organisation. However policing is policing and the gifts and skills of times gone by are still of value today.

'What is truth?' Pontius Pilate asked Jesus 2000 years ago. We still struggle with that question. Is truth an unchangeable objective reality, or is it simply a subjective perception? 'That might be true for you, but it's not true for me', is a refrain commonly heard. In this book, I have changed the names of people and places, apart from that, I have told the truth as I remember it. Some of the stories I have told many times over the years and my wife says that each time I tell them they are slightly embellished. What a thing to say! Slightly offended by this allegation, I reject the accusation, but bearing in mind subjective reality, I take no responsibility for the veracity of the content.

Chapter 1 Training

She lay on a cold white slab, no clothes, no sheet, no jewellery, no identity and for her pillow a wooden block. Just an old woman, but now not even that, simply a discarded shell of flesh and bone, a lump of meat waiting for the attention of the Pathologist before disposal. Something like 80% of deaths occur in hospital, out of sight and perhaps even out of mind, the reality denied, euphemisms employed, the process sanitised. Few people have ever seen death in some of its more unpleasant faces. For most of us, the report of a fatal road accident conjures no particular mental picture, unless you have seen the mutilation high speed steel can do to the human body. I had seen death on TV, at the cinema, on videos and the like, but never confronted its reality until that day at the mortuary.

The Mortician prepared the body. Taking a scalpel, he cut from throat to groin, and then he pared back the skin from the ribs before using a saw to slice through the bone to expose the organs. He fetched a tin cup, gathered her blood, and poured it into a bowl until he was satisfied, and there she lay open and exposed, the smell of death and internal organs spreading round the room. There was a fan but it was not in use, as the Pathologist did not like the noise it made. In he came clad in protective clothing but no mask. 'Who have we here?' He asked, looking at me. 'Err, err, PC James Cannon is my name sir, sent here to watch a post mortem'. 'New boy are you?' 'Yes, sir, this is my first day'.

It was actually my second day, but my first day on shift work. I had joined the Police some months before. The selection process took many months and involved interviews, form filling and physical tests plus an examination if the applicant was not sufficiently academically qualified. I told them that I held an Ordinary National Certificate (ONC) in Business Studies. They had never heard of an ONC. I pointed out that it had taken me two years at night school to pass and it was worth two or three A level GCE's. The recruiting Sergeant replied; 'well if it's that good you won't have any problems with the exam will you.'

Thus I had to go into Brightstone Police Station and sit the exam, which fortunately for me, I passed well enough. Around 150 people had originally applied at the same time as I did. Several months later when we presented ourselves at police HQ for the final interview with the Chief Constable there were only 12 of us left. The others had been whittled away by interview, exams, health problems, skeletons in the cupboard and the like. It always makes me bristle slightly when people say it is easy to join the police. It wasn't then and it isn't now.

So there we were, the 12 of us at Headquarters for an interview with the Chief Constable. He had been a Chief Constable for about 30 years, and was now nearing retirement. We were taken to an office near the Chief Constable's office and told to call him sir and stand at attention; I knew that meant that we had to be smart, but little beyond that. We were then paraded outside his office.

Instructions given, in we went, one at a time. I was kept standing smartly throughout the interview. He looked up at me and the conversation went something like this. 'Your name is Cannon,' 'yes, sir.' 'And you live in Brightstone?' 'Yes sir.' 'And you have a wife and no children?' 'Yes, sir.' 'What does your wife think about you applying for the police?' 'She's very happy about it sir.' 'Why do you want to be a Police Officer?' 'I want to do something useful and constructive sir.' 'I see you have already had six jobs and you are only 22 years old, why?' 'Well sir, I have changed each job for a better one and I hope and believe this will be the best of all.' 'What do you have to offer the Police Force?' 'I've wanted to join since I was a small boy, I regard it as a calling, I believe in justice, I'm honest and keen and willing to learn, and I'm not afraid of hard work.' 'It will require a lot of hard work to make the grade. Do you think you're up to it?' 'Yes sir, I do.' 'Very well Mr Cannon we will have to see.' I was out in a little under four minutes as were all the candidates. The 12 of us were taken to another room for a nerve-racking wait. Finally the Training Officer came in to tell us that eight of us were in and four had been turned down, all on the basis of some four minutes with the Chief Constable after all the other tests and interviews.

So it was that on a rainy November morning in 1971 I presented myself to Police Headquarters to begin the great adventure. I wanted to do well, I was determined to work hard, study hard and rather fancied myself as making it to Chief Constable, if not Commissioner of the Metropolitan Police, making a real difference to society, finding out what changes the Police Force needed to make and fearlessly implementing them. I kept all this to myself of course, humility was the order of the day. Uniforms were issued and our photographs were taken for the preparation of our warrant cards. Then we were taken to the Magistrates Court to swear allegiance to the Queen and her officers. We were now ready to begin our training. Training began with a residential induction week at Headquarters. We were issued with uniforms and told what Larkshire Constabulary expected of us. Then it was off to Burrstone near the coast for 13 weeks of residential training.

I had passed my driving test just a week or so before my appointment and had purchased a 1959 Morris Minor for the princely sum of £110. I was very hesitant because I had found little time for any driving, and I knew that I very much needed some practice. I had only had 12 lessons and my driving instructor had felt that I was far from ready and advised against taking the test. However, I wanted to pass before I joined the Police so I went ahead, took the test and somehow passed. The instructor was obviously rather surprised and worried, and wouldn't even let me drive home from the testing Station. I had never driven in the dark before the 50-mile journey to the regional training centre one dark winter night, and I found it very difficult but got there safely. I parked the car in the Training Centre car park, and I had very few opportunities to use it while training there.

Every so often, I think it was four weekly, we were allowed a weekend leave and one Friday afternoon I set out for the journey home. In a built up area I approached a set of traffic lights. There were three lanes with arrows on the road indicating left, straight ahead and right. I wanted to go straight ahead so I positioned myself in the middle lane with vehicles on either side of me. When the lights changed, I drove off, concentrating on my driving. I hardly noticed the van on my left who should be turning left but instead wanted to go straight ahead and was forced to wait for me and pull in behind. He was obviously greatly annoyed and as we left the built up area he overtook and then swerved in front of me and braked sharply. I had to swerve off the road and brake fiercely.

Now my blood was up and I pursued him, flashing my lights and sounding the horn. After we had driven a little way out of the built up area the van stopped. Three men got out and advanced on me looking very menacing, one of them rolling up his sleeves. I got out and could see I was in a spot of bother! However now I was a police officer, I might know very little, but I was an officer of the law. I pulled out my pristine new warrant card and trying to sound confident, brandished the card, saying that I wanted a word with them about their driving. To my immense satisfaction and relief, their menacing attitude immediately melted away, they became conciliatory and apologetic and we parted amicably enough, after they had been duly advised. I came to learn that warrant cards had a profound effect in such situations, usually positive, but sometimes red rag to a bull.

The 13 weeks of training passed in a blur of learning the definitions of Theft, Firearms, Burglary, Forgery etc, etc; there were about 100 definitions and we had to learn a few each week and then demonstrate that we had learned them in a test each Monday morning. After all this time, I can still remember some of them today. We suffered drills with an immaculately turned out Sergeant, shouting his orders, the peak of his cap slit to make him look fiercer. There were endless hours of classroom instruction on countless aspects of the law, whom we could arrest, when we could arrest, what to look for, what to say in court, what not to say in court and so on. We had exercises on simulated accidents, public order situations, major crime, traffic control, giving evidence and the like, and we had keep fit classes and self defence training.

Self-defence training was led by a small man who looked as if a gust of wind would blow him over. We stood opposite him in our T-shirts, shorts and plimsolls and he looked us up and down. Approaching me he said, 'do you think you're stronger than me?' I don't know why he picked on me, anyway trying to be humble I replied, 'I wouldn't like to say, sir.' 'What do you mean - you wouldn't like to say, sir? Do you think you're stronger than me or not?' 'Well sir, it's hard to tell.' 'Yes or no' he shouted. 'Well yes then'

I said firmly and foolishly. 'Right, let's see shall we? Grab me and put me down on the deck.' 'I wouldn't want to hurt you sir.' 'Do as you're told, boy.' 'Yes sir.' With that, I grabbed for him and for a second I felt his strength and thought, I am stronger, and then, stronger or not, I was flying through the air to land painfully on my back. 'We'll have to teach you how to fall lad, won't we?' He smiled down at me.

We were taught how to fall, how to tackle someone armed with a knife, how to arrest and use a number of restraining holds, especially one called the hammer lock and bar, how to use a truncheon, how to make an arrest, how to defend ourselves in other situations and so on. We practised on each other and had great fun throwing one another about. The training was of limited value unless the skills were practised regularly and developed, which most of us intended to do, but few of us actually did.

The physical training involved the usual sort of circuit training together with running, often off the College grounds into Burrstone and round the streets. We were 'promised' the run of runs towards the end of the course, up and over what was called Pompey's Hill which ran along the coast, a run of more than 10 miles. We soon learned that Pompey's Hill was infamous for its difficulty and ability to inflict pain on the fittest recruit. We really looked forward to the run! The pain and difficulty of it was frequently emphasised and expectation deliberately heightened by the instructors.

We were a disparate lot. In age, we varied between 19 and 37. In height from 5'8" to 6'6". In background, ex-military forces, ex-police cadets, clerks, a professional athlete, engineers, butchers, bakers and candlestick makers. One or two really did look forward to the run at Pompey's Hill, particularly the ex-professional athlete who was after breaking the record time - he had been forced to give up his athletic career by an injury. The rest of us simply wanted to survive!

When the great day came, we donned our T-shirts, shorts and plimsolls and set off on a cold murky winter's day. The ex-athlete streaked away and was soon lost to sight. We plodded on, looking in horror at Pompey's Hill as it loomed up in front of us out of the mist. We ran and scrabbled over the hill, gasping for breath and trying to ignore the pain. College Instructors were stationed at various points to encourage us on and make sure there was no slacking. After an hour or so of pain and effort, the 10-mile run was completed. I did pretty well and was pleased with myself.

To our surprise, there was no sign of our athlete. We enquired and determined that he had not arrived at the finish line. He eventually turned up having taken a wrong turning and run miles out of his way! He was devastated, absolutely inconsolable and he slunk off. We never saw him again. Apparently, he was so upset that he made an attempt on his life, how serious it was we were never told. Thankfully, he survived, but he was obviously deemed unsuitable and was sent packing back to his force and out of the police.

We lost one or two more as the course progressed. Sometimes the study proved too much, occasionally behaviour fell short of the standards demanded and some found that they just were not cut out for the life of a police officer. What would it be like? We knew that it wouldn't be like the acted out scenes that we were trained in. Would we be brave enough when faced with real violence? Would we be wise enough to defuse some of the situations that we would encounter? Would we be blessed with a 'copper's nose', the ability some officers have to spot a criminal where others would see nothing? We would be on probation for two years, could we cope? Time alone would tell, and most of us were blessed with the confidence of youth, with our embryonic abilities we would make it.

Every so often, there was a dance at the college and girls were invited from a local nursing home. The married men, as I was, soon got off with the girls, only for a dance you understand, but we seemed to fear rejection less than the hesitant single men gathering their courage to chance their arm. If not on guard duty or other tasks we were allowed out of the grounds in our free time, we had to be back in by 2230 hours when the building was locked.

When allowed out we usually made straight for the local hostelries, and got back on time on every occasion, bar one. On this occasion we had such a good time, and probably so much to drink, that we overlooked the time and came back to find that the building was all locked up. If we were caught by the duty Instructor, we would be in hot water and up before the Commandant in the morning. The need for self-discipline had been heavily emphasised and a very dim view would be taken of our transgression. We went quietly round the building and found a first floor window open. We shinned up a drainpipe and got in without being detected. Giggling like school girls, we crept along to the dormitory and got safely to bed. Whew!

The training at Burrstone concluded with a parade to which families and guests were invited. In preparation we spent regular time on the drill square learning to march and turn to order, square bashing as I believe it's called in military circles. The ex-military men were well used to this and were appointed as squad leaders to keep the rest of us in order. We more or less got the hang of it with enough practice.

When the day came, we all dressed in best uniform, hair cut short, boots bulled until they gleamed, and marched onto the parade square with guests and family all around. An Assistant Chief Constable from Larkshire inspected us under the watchful eye of our Drill Sergeant, and then we had to demonstrate some of our marching skills. We all kept in reasonable formation and I managed to turn correctly and stand at attention at the right moment. Our display concluded with a march past our dignitaries, eyes right and all that. As we did the march past, I managed to get out of step. I tried desperately to get back into step, looking as if I wanted to do the foxtrot instead of a quick march! I managed it eventually red faced and humbled, the only one to make a fool of himself. The Drill Sergeant gave me one of his looks as we left the parade ground and made some remark about two left feet. I ignored it and tried to look relaxed and unfazed by the incident. How did I manage to do that, what a plonker as Dell boy would say!

The time there passed, I did well with my studies and was happy with my posting to Brightstone, the county town of Larkshire. I was very fortunate with this posting. During my first week at Police Headquarters, a senior civilian spoke to me. He wanted to know where I lived. My wife and I had bought a flat in Brightstone, we were happy there and planned to stay for some time. Despite my protestations, he was adamant that a flat was not suitable accommodation for a police officer; I must sell it and move into a police house. I rang my wife and told her the news. She was really upset and asked it there was any way round it, I didn't think there was. I couldn't see her to talk face to face and the phone call ended with me upset and her in tears.

My face obviously betrayed my distress and one of the Training Inspectors asked me what the matter was. I told him and he went and got my file and arranged for me to be posted to Brightstone so that I could keep the flat. I was very grateful and my wife was greatly relieved. It gave me a good measure of peace of mind knowing my posting when everyone else had to wait about nine weeks before they were told. The importance of the decision to keep our flat was amply demonstrated when the housing market took off and we were in it. Later many of my colleagues who had moved into police houses found that they had great difficulty in finding the money to buy a property.

The initial training was quite intensive and all consuming. The confines of the Training School became our little world, and the events outside of limited consequence and interest. At the end of the 13 weeks there, we returned to Headquarters for a further two residential weeks of familiarisation with local force procedures. Finally, after 16 weeks, we had completed our initial training and were ready for all that lay ahead.

Chapter 2 First days

I was instructed to report to Brightstone Police Station at 0900 on my first day. I walked to work clad in my shiny new uniform, hoping and praying that no one would ask me any questions, my head might be full of theory but I was only too aware of how short I was on experience. I felt very conscious of the looks and occasional stares, and sought to give the appearance of confidence and self-assuredness while conveying the impression that I was not to be troubled. I made it to within a few hundred yards of the Police Station when a man ran up to me calling; 'Help, help Officer, there's been an accident!' My heart sank, my mind went blank and as I walked back with him I thought furiously how I could extricate myself from this nightmare.

I arrived at the scene, where I found two damaged cars, traffic stopped, drivers and passengers gathered round, and everyone looking for the long arm of the law to dispense wisdom and justice, and all they got was me! My mind remained completely blank, I dithered, and I walked round the scene hoping it looked as if I was undertaking an important evaluation exercise. I cleared my throat, several times, and then I heard music to my ears, the sounds of a police siren, the cavalry were here! Experienced officers sent me packing and took over. Greatly relieved I continued on my way and reported for duty just on time.

Much of my first day was spent familiarising myself with the Police Station, meeting various officers, finding a locker and sorting out which was to be my section and what duties I would be on. There were four sections, each led by an Inspector, with two Sergeants and around fifteen Constables. We worked a three-shift system 0600 - 1400 early shift, 1400 - 2200 late shift and 2200 - 0600 night shift. We worked seven days on each shift with two days off in between; there was just one weekend off a month, when we had an extra days leave.

For each shift, we were expected to parade for duty 15 minutes before the starting time, unpaid, in order to be out on the streets promptly. When I had been sorted out on that first day, I was able to go out for a brief ride in a police car. I listened to the radio crackling away sending patrols here and there but our car was left untroubled and, disappointingly for me at least, nothing happened before I went off duty at 1700. Thankfully, I made the walk home without encountering any further problems.

My second day began at 0430, struggling up from sleep to dress and walk to the Police Station in time for 0545 Parade. I met the Section Sergeant, a very smart ex-military man with a wonderful handlebar moustache. The first question he asked me was how much I weighed. When I told him, he replied, 'good, you're in the tug of war team.' I was later to find out what that meant. The parade was reassuringly relaxed and we sat around a large table and were told of the crimes that had happened overnight and the vehicles and people we were to keep an eye out for. Duties were then allocated.

I was put with an experienced officer, Mike, and told to have breakfast at 0900 and attend a post mortem at 1000. That afforded great hilarity to the shift and I was treated to a number of frighteningly gory descriptions of what I would face. I learned later that they were being quite nice to me really. One poor lad was deemed a little too cocky and needed a lesson. On the day he was to attend a post mortem his sandwich box was appropriated and his cheese and cucumber sandwiches were replaced with raw offal, courtesy of a local butcher. For some reason or other, he wasn't very hungry after that!

On that first day for me, someone had told the Ambulance Service that a new boy was going to a pm and when I arrived at the Hospital Mortuary a number of ambulance men were there full of smiles and helpful comments like, 'Don't worry if you faint, we'll come and pick you up,' and 'If you're going to throw up the Pathologist gets quite upset if it goes over his shoes,' and 'don't forget to duck when he chucks organs in the scales, the blood goes everywhere'. My Sergeant had told me that I must look interested and listen carefully to the Pathologist as the procedure unfolded. As I took in the gruesome scene, I tried to look interested while keeping as far away as possible from the slab. The Pathologist began to cut out the organs, the heart, lungs, spleen etc, as each organ came out the Mortician put them into the scales and I had the job of weighing them and recording their weight, and do you know, I did have to duck as blood sprayed up the wall from the organs as they flopped into the scales!

The post mortem examination was on the old woman I mentioned at the beginning of the book. The old woman had suffered a broken hip and it was thought that she had died from shock following the injury. The Pathologist wasn't convinced of this so decided to look at her brain. Opening her head involved a scalpel followed by a circular saw, hammer and chisel and I was feeling decidedly green although morbidly fascinated. He extracted her brain and exclaimed in triumph. Amongst all the blood something was out of place, she had died of a brain haemorrhage. I obediently looked interested and he called me over, produced a bucket of brains, and pointed out the various maladies that had afflicted their owners!

I eventually escaped and stumbled out into the fresh air, offering a sickly smile to the grinning ambulance men as I went. For days afterwards, I dreamt of that old lady, I saw her poor worn out body, I smelt her blood and the unpleasant odour of internal organs and I ducked again as the blood spattered from her organs. However, I had survived. I had confronted death and my fears and I had coped. I was a little more prepared for some of the things that lay ahead.

I went back to the Police Station for some more leg pulling, had a cuppa and then went out on the road. For a while at least, I forgot the old lady and looked at the world with new eyes. Which cars looked worth stopping? Which of these people were actually big villains about to commit some terrible deed? What calls were we about to be sent on? Those and many other thoughts rushed through my mind as I plied my colleague with questions. It wasn't long before the radio crackled into life telling all patrols of a burglary that had just taken place and giving the description of a suspect. The hunt was on! The adrenaline pumped, I looked everywhere at once and just hoped that we might be the lucky ones to find him.

We were! Just a little while later we saw a man who fitted the description in the shopping centre. Mike recognised him as a known villain, so we left the car and approached him. As we did so I rehearsed everything I had been taught, the words, the self-defence moves, what to look for etc. Would he run, would he resist? In the event he came quietly, Mike said to him, 'Hello Fred, what have you been up to?' 'Me, nothing, why?' 'Been anywhere near Ladysmith Avenue have you?' 'Not me, I've been here shopping for hours.' 'Where is your shopping then?' 'Well, I haven't bought anything yet, have I?' 'I wonder what we'd find if we looked in your house and car?' 'You wouldn't find nothing' said a decidedly worried looking Fred. 'I think you've been at it, Fred and you're nicked on suspicion of burglary.' Hard as I thought, I couldn't remember that terminology in the Training Manual. As we were in a pedestrian precinct, I was entrusted with the task of walking him back to the Police Station while Mike drove back. I held my prisoners arm discreetly, trying to look nonchalant and in control.

Back at the Police Station, we processed him and my name went down on the charge sheet as joint arresting officer. An arrest on my first day, the beginning of a triumphant career! What a thrill it was, what adventures must lay ahead. I was less keen when it came to writing a statement. Mike dictated, 'My colleague PC Lemark said to him, "I am arresting you for the offence of burglary, you are not obliged to say anything unless you wish to do so, but whatever you say will be written down and may be given in evidence." ' I protested that this wasn't exactly what Mike had said. 'Write it down' he growled. 'But, but...' 'Look it means the same, write it down.' So I did. Was that a case of perjury on my first day I wondered? I soon learned that it is better to say the right things and if you don't it's better to tell the truth anyway.

The paperwork done and the prisoner passed to CID, we got back out on the road for the last hour or so, looking for the next villain, waiting for the next call. As 1400 approached, we returned to the Police Station, Mike pleased to be going home, me with a heavy heart that I would have to depart from the excitement, at least until the following morning. Still I had arrived; I was a real police officer. Bring on the future!

I had little trouble getting up the next day at 0430; I was excited and ready to go. Parade at 0545, they still called it parade and it wasn't so long before then that it would have been a proper parade, conducted standing, with uniform and equipment inspections. Much more relaxed to sit round the parade table while the Sergeant allocated our duties and told us of particular things to look out for. Then we were off in our little Hillman Imp driven by Mike - I wasn't allowed to drive a police car yet.

Among the cars to look out for were a Triumph Stag sports car and a Rolls Royce, both stolen from London and thought to be heading our way. They should be easy enough to spot one would think. We patrolled round our area, and later in the morning, we were driving round a quiet residential area when we saw the stolen cars parked and unattended. Checks revealed that a known car thief lived in the house outside of which the cars were parked. Obviously a very intelligent villain! We knocked on the door, got no reply, went round the back and got in. We searched the house and after a while, I opened the door of the cupboard under the stairs. There crouched the man we sought pointing a shotgun straight at me! 'The first bastard who comes near me gets this.' I got the message and hastily shut the door again and told Mike. He called for assistance.

In those days, it took ages to get a firearm-trained officer to the scene and we had to make do with some more unarmed officers complete with truncheons and a police dog. The handler was not at all keen on putting his dog at risk, but we all felt that our lives were more important than the dog and he should go in first. 'Look we've got no guns, the first person he sees could get shot and its better that a bloody dog gets shot than one of us.' 'Sod you, I'd rather have my dog than any of you lot.' Eventually he reluctantly agreed but made it quite clear to the man in the cupboard that there would be hell to pay if he shot his dog. 'Listen you bastard, I have a dog here, a big, angry, vicious fucking dog. I suggest you give up that gun cos if you shoot my dog, I'll fucking tear you apart limb from limb and feed your bits to the other dogs'. Then the door was opened and the man was confronted with 80lbs of snarling teeth and muscle straining at the leash. He gave up immediately to everyone's relief and was dragged off to the cells. A burglar on my first day and an armed man on the second, what would be next!

The remaining two days of the week passed without any major adventures, although every call was an adventure to me. We stopped some cars and I worked on talking to people, checking their documents, learning what made people worth checking. I reported my first offender, the driver of a car failing to display a tax disc. He told me that it was in the post but at my request produced his Driving Licence, MOT and Insurance. I pointed out that if his tax application was indeed in the post he would have to include his MOT and Insurance. He replied, 'it's a fair cop, guv.' I was horrified. No one said that except in old Ealing movies and the Magistrates would surely think that I had made it up. In the event he pleaded guilty and saved me from any doubts the Magistrates might have displayed.

Early shift led to our one weekend a month off, a long weekend from 1400 on Friday until nights on Tuesday. These weekends became very precious. They were the only opportunity to keep up social contacts and really relax. The time off between other shifts was very short and not long enough to do much. I overcame this to a certain extent by adopting the Sergeant's advice to be prepared to socialise on early turn. It was only a week to survive of getting up at 0430. Once the initial excitement of going on duty passed, I hated the getting up and longed for a Saturday lie in. In order that I could fully appreciate a lie in, I set the alarm for 0430 on Saturday morning so that I could get up, turn it off and go back to bed. Bliss!

Nights came round soon enough and I reported for duty at 2145, my stomach knotted with excitement about what might await me. I went out with several senior colleagues who were very different in their characters and methods. Mike was cheerful and humorous with the people we met which seemed to put people at their ease. He had about four years service under his belt, which equated to a man of great experience, at least in my view. I also went out with Paul, a man of over 20 years experience who had been on CID for a number of years before getting into some kind of trouble and being sent back to uniform. Paul was very cynical, liked a drink and was prone to violence. We stopped a motorcyclist one night and Paul asked his name. 'Mickey Mouse' was the reply. A smack round the ear from Paul followed. 'Now tell me' and he did. On nights we went back to the Police Station at 0400 for a cuppa, but not Paul, he took me to one of the Breweries and had what he called, 'cold tea'!

At that time, there were two Breweries in the town, one right in the town centre. The Breweries were very pleased to welcome police visitors during the night as it was good crime prevention, and they allocated supplies of 'cold tea' for us. In the rural area, I came across the odd farm where the farmer too welcomed police visits during the night and left out a flagon of cider for nocturnal visitors to enjoy. Powerful stuff that cider, and very unwise of anyone to have more than one glass. It was very rare for these alcoholic 'tea stops' to be abused. They suited both parties, most of us were aware that we needed to keep our senses about us and there was always the danger of the Sergeant or Inspector catching you out which could result in very severe trouble!

I was very surprised to come across the Sergeant one night, feet up in the Brewery enjoying a cup of `cold tea`. I came to see that there was tremendous camaraderie and these stops enhanced that fellowship. The group of men I worked with, the Section as it was called, arrested more people than all the other three sections put together, so something was working. We mixed socially as well and I became good friends with some of them.

Nights were usually very busy for the first few hours and then tailed off. Some of the officers really struggled to keep awake and whatever their duties managed to find somewhere to snooze. It was easy enough in a patrol car but foot patrol was a different matter, nowhere was open and snoozing in the open was not on. However, the town boasted three railway Stations and one of them always had a train in the sidings, unlocked, nicely heated and very comfortable. So comfortable that it was easy to fall fast asleep and not notice that the train had moved off early in the morning! More than once searches were launched for missing foot patrol officers who eventually turned up at Fireford, 20 odd miles away, or even down on the coast. Thankfully, I never fell asleep on nights; I was too keen and eager.

I found the early shift the killer, getting up at 0430 or so just didn't seem natural. One morning when I was feeling particularly tired I found a nice peaceful field soon after 0600, and was having a quiet zzz when the farmer came by and vigorously banged on the roof of the car to wish me a cheerful 'good morning'. When I had climbed back down off the car roof, I returned the greeting. No peace for the wicked!

Nights were very different from day duties in many respects. The work tended to concentrate around accidents, fights and drunkenness in the early part of the night, followed by the luxury of time to look for crime in the wee small hours. In the daytime, an officer is expected to be visible, to walk on the outside of the pavement so that everyone can see his reassuring presence. At night, we sought the shadows and were quiet, often pausing to listen for sounds that carry far in the silence of the night. I liked the peace and quiet. We clambered up on roofs at the back of the shopping areas, checked the security of premises on our beat, tried to guess where crime might be taking place and dreamt of catching a burglar red handed. If a break-in on our beat was discovered the next day, we were likely to be called in to explain why we hadn't found it. The stock answer was that it must have happened after 0600. It wasn't very convincing.

If I was very fortunate, I was allowed to crew the emergency vehicle for an hour or so while the regular crew were in the Station having something to eat. This was the chance for real action, and the odd car chase or exciting call was great fun. During my first six weeks a senior colleague always accompanied me, our duties were split between foot patrol and mobile patrol, and I thoroughly enjoyed it and gained some confidence that I had learned a number of important lessons.

One night around 0230, we were driving on the outskirts of the town when we saw a car being driven into the town at some speed. We didn't actually check the speed but we stopped the car to check it and advise the driver. My experienced colleague did the talking. 'Where are you going in such a hurry?' 'Home'. 'Where's home?' An address was duly provided. 'Where have you been?' 'None of your business.' This was the first time I had encountered such a response and I began racking my brains for the right way to deal with this. 'Would you mind opening your boot?' 'Yes I would, why do you want to look in there?' 'You were travelling at high speed through the town in the middle of the night, you won't tell us where you have been and I want to see if you've been up to no good.' 'Well I'm telling you that I haven't. I'm a perfectly respectable citizen minding my own business in a law abiding way. If you suspect that I have done something wrong you had better do what you need to do, otherwise don't bother me any further and get out of my way!' There was a lengthy pause as my colleague considered his options. 'I want to see your driving documents.' 'Will that make you feel better if you can be a bloody nuisance?' He produced his documents, which were all in order. 'Well, all done now, I intend to continue home and you can go and bother some other innocent member of the public.' He got into his car and threw out the cigarette he had been smoking. 'That's litter, pick it up' said my colleague. 'Pleased with your cheap victory are you?' said our motorist as he got out and picked up the cigarette. We watched as he drove off.

We discussed what had happened. My colleague was of the opinion that we did not really have any reasonable suspicion that he had done anything wrong and therefore had to back down. He did say that in his experience people like that would come to our attention again in some way or other and maybe then we would have the opportunity to take action against him. He told me of a previous experience of a similar nature. Some years before he had bought a 56lb bag of potatoes. As it was too heavy to carry back to his car, he left it at the shop, went to get his car and parked outside while he collected them. As he went to go into the shop a Traffic Warden approached and told him he couldn't park there. He explained the situation but the Warden would have none of it and said if he didn't move the car immediately he would book him. My friend had no option but to obey. He never forgot that Warden and some years later while on patrol he saw the Warden out driving his car. He stopped the car, went over it with a fine toothcomb and took great pleasure in booking him for a number of offences. In my imagination, I saw the satisfaction of the scene and hoped I might have that opportunity with our motoring friend!

Chapter 3 On My Own

After six weeks of being tutored by experienced officers, I was allowed out on my own. At first on foot patrol, walking the beat, growing in confidence as experience built and challenges were successfully met. There was still much learning to do and I made many mistakes, some of which could have got me into a lot of trouble. I found that the frustration with foot patrol was that unless you were very lucky there was little chance of being able to attend the calls. They were allocated to mobile patrols and even if the call was to somewhere in the town centre, a car invariably got there before I did. Nevertheless, it had its compensations. I enjoyed getting to know people, finding shops where I was welcome for a cuppa and a chat, learning where problems might occur, which shops most often suffered from shoplifting and I also enjoyed standing on the corner watching all the girls go by. I was only looking, honestly.

It was also useful to find out which pubs were likely to have trouble. Some of them catered for the barristers and solicitors at the Crown Court and were never any trouble. Others catered for officer workers and again were rarely the source of any trouble. Others catered for the heavy drinkers, trouble makers and the like. They were frequently the source of trouble. I asked the Landlord of one such pub why he seemed to attract such a clientele. 'If I attract the office wallahs they come in, buy half of shandy and make that last all lunch hour. If I attract the people who are in there now, they drink four or five pints in an hour, some even more. So it's well worth the risk of the odd punch-up'. I suppose he had a point!

On the first night on my own, my beat was in the town centre and around 0300 I was walking along the main shopping street. At that time of night the town is eerily quiet, nothing moves and every sound seems far louder than usual. In accordance with my training, I was walking quietly in and out of the shadows, stopping to listen at regular intervals and feeling quite tense.

As I passed a Jeweller's I thought I heard something. I stopped to listen and heard voices whispering, the voices were coming from the roof of the three-storey building. Trying to sound calm but with my heart thumping with excitement I called in, whispering into the radio to report what I had heard. I was told that backup was on the way, and as the suspected intruders couldn't get down the front of the building I was to go round the back, climb up on the roof and attempt to apprehend them knowing that help would be there within minutes. I don't like heights and I certainly didn't relish the thought of having to struggle with at least two villains on a roof in the dark. However, duty was duty and I went round the back and as quietly and carefully as I could went up a fire escape and onto the roof. I crept forward expecting the confrontation at any moment. My mouth was dry, the adrenaline was pumping, eyes and ears straining in the dark and every sense heightened.

As I edged towards the front of the building, there was a commotion in the street below. I looked over the top and saw Policemen running and shouting, heading towards the back of the building. The villains must have got out somewhere. Desperate to be part of the action I made my way back down as quickly as I could. On my descent, I found myself confronted with a row of grinning Policemen. My dear colleagues had just treated me to my 'induction'. I was shaking like a leaf and wrung out by the experience and it took a little while before I could share their 'joke'. Of course the more indignant I was the funnier they found it. I had no idea what was coming and was unaware of this 'local custom'. I could have fallen I guess, but 'what if' was not worth pursuing. The custom continued but we did always try to make sure the joke was safe, it would be very hard to explain what had happened if there was an accident.

As in every town, there was an element of youths apparently always bent on causing trouble. These local yobs soon learned that there was a sprog copper around and revelled in the opportunity of having a laugh at my expense. Name-calling, jeers when I dealt with someone, giving advice to people as sort of barrack room lawyers, threats and challenges were all their stock in trade. As is so often the case they were very brave in the group but much less so when I encountered them on their own. Their abuse and mickey taking was a real source of irritation and I grew increasingly angry and looked for an opportunity to take some positive action. It also meant that I couldn't go in the town off duty in the evening, especially with my wife. All the time I worked there, we had to miss out on the joys of Brightstone's nightlife, such as it was. It just wasn't worth the bother and the potential aggravation

One evening when I was patrolling the town centre, they were worse than usual with the taunts and threats and my patience was wearing thin, in my eyes it wasn't just me they were insulting, they were making the whole of the Police Service look foolish and impotent in the minds of passing members of the public. Talking to them proved a waste of time, I was not sure enough of myself to arrest them for public order offences, and I was reluctant to admit my lack of knowledge. Finally, one of them approached a police car and began to let the tyres down encouraged by his mates. The police car was parked in a taxi rank in the middle of a busy town centre road and I was on the opposite pavement. Something snapped inside me and I ran across the road, he stood up at my approach and I delivered a good right hook which deposited him on his backside in the middle of the road causing the traffic to come shuddering to a stop to avoid running him over. I was horrified at what I'd done, but he got up, ran off and all his mates fled with him. Motorists wound down their windows, not to complain, but to congratulate me, 'Well done mate, they could do with a bit more of that', 'good to see the strong arm of the law in action' etc. The youth never complained and many of them learned a healthy respect, which curbed their behaviour, at least when they were within range!

That action could have cost me my job and even led to a court appearance. I was very grateful and relieved to have got away with it and made a mental note to try, whatever the provocation, to keep my temper under control.

Despite my inexperience of driving, I was very keen to drive a police car. Driving courses were regularly held at the Driving School at Headquarters and I applied to go on one. It seemed that I would have to wait a very long time so I applied just to take a police-driving test. I was given a date and duly reported to Headquarters Driving School. In those days, the Police used Hillman Imps as panda cars and Ford Escort Estates as emergency vehicles. Only the Traffic Department had bigger and more powerful cars, and there was no way we would get our hands on one of them. I expected to be asked to drive an Imp or an Escort but to my horror, I found myself in a Bedford Van with column gears. I had never driven a large van before and never encountered column gears. I was allowed just a few minutes in the yard to familiarise myself with the controls.

I don't know how I did it but I passed, I think I had bemoaned my fate so much that the instructor took pity on me. He did make a recommendation that I go on a course as soon as possible! There were six grades of driving permit, from the prestigious grade 1 to the humble grade 6. I was given a grade 6. The grade indicated the types of cars one could drive and I was just very happy to have a permit of whatever grade. I never did go on a driving course and was still a grade 6 driver when I left.

Having a permit didn't mean that I was going to drive very often; I was the new boy and would be on the beat most of the time while I waited my turn. Finally, on one early shift I was allowed out on patrol in one of the Hillman Imps. What joy! I whizzed around my patrol area and then proudly drove through the town centre on a busy morning. At a particularly busy intersection, I was just negotiating the bend when there was a very strange and very loud grinding noise from the car. I reluctantly had to stop immediately to see what on earth had happened. The traffic built up, people stopped to look. I got out to see oil spreading in all directions from under the car. In the middle of this pool of oil lay the sump, which had just dropped off! One very embarrassed Policeman had to call for help; the car wasn't driveable so I had to wait until a low loader came to take the car away.

Then I walked back to the Police Station to face the Sergeant, who wanted to know what I had done to the car. I protested vigorously that I had not hit any bumps, nor been off road and had done nothing to cause the damage. I hope he believed me but I didn't get to drive again for quite a while. I suspect someone had been having some fun on nights and hadn't admitted what they'd done. Another lesson learned, check the car thoroughly before taking it out, although looking underneath was far from easy!

It was night duty when I had another opportunity to drive a police car again. One night I was patrolling round an industrial estate and got out of the car to check a factory, which I found to be insecure. I informed the Station and told them that I was going in to check around. The factory led into a large high warehouse, which was full of large wooden crates. I clambered over the crates to see if anyone was hiding there. As I reached the very top of the pile, my car keys, the police car keys, fell out of my pocket and in between the crates. I tried to reach them but there was no way of getting to them without removing a large number of heavy crates, which I couldn't move on my own. By that time, the Sergeant and another officer had arrived; we searched the premises, which appeared all in order. It was then time for me to reluctantly admit my predicament and ask for help. The Sergeant was not best pleased, he called for more help and for something like an hour, we huffed and puffed as we moved a large number of those heavy crates to reach the keys. Eventually successful the Sergeant looked at me and said, 'well Cannon, you're certainly making your mark now that you are driving police cars, I wonder what you'll get up to next?' I promised to be extra careful in future, and I did manage not to lose the car keys again! The incident cost me a pint all round and made me the subject of my colleagues humour until the next person made a cock-up.

Hillman Imps as patrol vehicles were okay I guess, all 950cc of them, or was it 850cc? However, it would have been nice to have a big powerful car. The town youths believed that our cars had been tuned up so that they performed like a much more powerful car. We did nothing to dissuade them from that view; in fact, we actively encouraged it.

One night duty on foot patrol I came across a beautiful Jaguar parked in amongst the Ford Anglia's, Vauxhall Cresta's and Ford Escort's of a typical estate. I did a check on it and found that it had been reported stolen. The keys were still in the ignition and it seemed clear that it had been abandoned because it had run out of petrol. I was determined to drive it back to the Police Station. So I went to the Station pump and got a gallon of two star petrol, which I duly put into the Jaguar's tank. It was an XJ6, a 5.3 litre V12. I turned the key, nothing seemed to happen and I feared that it wouldn't start. However when I got out of the car I found that the engine was running, but it was so quiet that I didn't realise, not quite like my Morris Minor! The Jag only pinked slightly on the two star. Then I enjoyed the trip back to the Station. I should have known the way by then but somehow I got lost and took a long way round. In the Station yard, I delighted in power steering, which I had never encountered before, it made manoeuvring easier than for a Hillman Imp. I parked the Jag in the Superintendent's parking bay to await the owner. Great fun, I hope the two star didn't do it any lasting damage.

When I did get another go in a police car (back to a Hillman Imp), I was given my very first call. It was to an edge of town estate where someone was complaining that a neighbour had injured their cat. Heady stuff, eh! Nevertheless I went there with due dispatch and determined the circumstances. Apparently, the alleged offender had a pond in his garden containing goldfish. The complainant's cat had taken a shine to the goldfish and eaten a couple.

The offender didn't resort to shooting the cat at first; instead he tried to cover the pond with netting to keep the cat away. It soon became clear that a little netting was not going to do the job. The next time that the offender saw the cat approaching his pond, he got his air rifle and shot the cat. The pellet had hit the cat in the face knocking out an eye, travelled on through its head and lodged in its neck close to the spine. Amazingly, the cat was still alive and made a complete recovery after an operation to replace its eye in the socket and remove the pellet.

I interviewed the neighbour, who readily confessed the deed. I confiscated his rifle and reported him for summons under an Act of Parliament from around 1911. He was quite indignant that he couldn't go around shooting the neighbour's cat while it was causing problems on his property, but you can't and that's that!

I came away from the scene feeling I had dealt capably with that problem and gained a little more confidence that I could deal with whatever might lay ahead. I also asked myself what I would have done if I had been in the offender's shoes? I convinced myself that I would have used my air rifle to frighten the cat, but not shoot it. Well I think so anyway. I also reasoned that a good criterion for me to employ was to take action against people for doing things I wouldn't do, but if they had done things I would do, I needed to think first and perhaps caution rather than report. I detest hypocrisy but have to acknowledge that we are all hypocritical to some extent. I can't claim that I have never made mistakes that could have caused an accident, or exceeded the speed limit or even, especially in my younger days, driven home when I was probably over the limit. I did such things rarely and tried not to. I knew a few officers who would drink to excess and drive regularly, and then when on duty arrest drivers for the same thing with great regularity, and seemed to think nothing of it.

Early on in my driving experience I was on nights enjoying myself looking for criminals when I saw a car being driven erratically, I followed it for a short while and felt confident that the driver must be under the influence of drink or drugs and decided to stop him. With the adrenaline flowing I saw a short stretch of clear road, sufficient to get by him, so I accelerated my Imp, went past him and cut in front of him, while waving him down. Unfortunately, I cut in too sharply, caught my bumper in his and pulled them both off. Oops! If the Sergeant or Inspector got to know, I would be in trouble and quite possibly be prosecuted in court. I spoke to the unhappy driver who was quite aggressive and indignant. He became a lot more conciliatory when I questioned him about his drinking. He lived nearby and in the end we did a deal. He would say nothing about my driving and I would say nothing about his drinking. We collected up our respective bumpers, put them in our cars and drove off. Not for the last time, I adjourned to a colleague's house where we straightened out the bumper and put it back on. It looked perfect, well almost. More care needed James!

Over the following weeks I got to know the town very well, the names of the roads, points of interest, the alleys, parks, shops and the areas where groups of villains lived and where trouble was likely to come. There was a variety of housing, from the grand large houses with lovely big cars in the drive, to the tatty back-street terraced houses where decaying bangers competed for space in the kerb outside. It is a sad fact that most of the crime that we know of is committed by the have-nots with the poor cars and living in the tatty housing. Over the years, I have learned that crime is committed probably just as frequently by the well off. They are just better at getting away with it or committing it within a culture that does not recognise dishonesty for what it is. Insider dealing, use of office equipment, fiddling of expenses, sweeteners for arranging a deal are all part of life's rich pattern for some who consider themselves honest and savagely condemn the burglar, common thief or joy rider.

Among the calls I was sent to, were quite a few domestic disputes, usually between husband and wife. As a young officer, I found it quite difficult trying to give advice to people as old, or older, than my parents. I did my best but soon learned two useful techniques for dealing with them. If I was feeling ready to take burdens on, I would have both of the participants together, take the side of one of them, and be quite critical to the other. Almost every time the other party would come to the aid of their criticised partner and the anger of both of them was turned on me. I would beat a retreat leaving them unhappy about my involvement but united and hopefully happy together. I'd like to think they would reflect on things and come to understand what I had done.

The other technique was to separate them, listen to each story and indicate carefully, without actually saying so, to each of them that I understood and was on their side. Then I would talk to them of the need to help others who weren't as wise as they were and from their moral high ground to be merciful to others. When I had done that to all involved and with a little good fortune, calm would return and they each would be feeling smug because their view had been respected. What happened after I left is a different matter, but I was rarely called back.

Perhaps inevitably we got to be regulars at some addresses. At one house, regular arguments broke out between husband and wife and she would throw things at him. The first time I went there, she had thrown his dinner over him, and flowerpots, crockery and anything to hand followed on subsequent occasions. The woman clearly was mentally disturbed and quite difficult to talk to. Each time there was an eruption the husband retreated to the local pub, and I couldn't blame him for that! I adopted the practice of going there and when she started with all her problems accompanied by tears and screams, saying, 'hang on, before you tell me all the problems, how about making me a cup of tea and then we can sit down and talk.' It did calm her down and she didn't make a bad cuppa. The Doctor was regularly consulted but it seemed that nothing could be done. As well as her mental fragility, she also had a serious drink problem. This ultimately led to her death. Her husband left her and one day she lay on the bed after too much alcohol, her cigarette ignited the mattress and she was burnt to death. A sorry end to the poor lady.

People have very different values and were a constant source of amazement to me. I remember visiting one particular house on a council estate. Inside the house was a real tip, wallpaper and paint was peeling off the walls, the carpets were worn and threadbare, the ceiling stained yellow by cigarette smoke. The children were in rags with dirty faces and snotty noses. Mum had a baby on her hip, a baby who definitely needed changing and was kept quiet with a dummy, mum's dress was old, torn and stained and a fag hung from her mouth. Dad was unshaven, unwashed, wearing old trousers and braces and wearing a string vest with too many holes in it, he too had a cigarette dangling from his mouth. Both parents punctuated their conversation with swearing and shouting at the children. In the kitchen, piles of unwashed dishes sat on the draining board and the waste bin overflowed with the remains of a curry.

Amidst all this, taking pride of place in the lounge was a large 26-inch television in a teak cabinet, at that time in the early 70's I had never seen a TV so big. Dad was busy drinking a beer while watching the racing, obviously hoping for his bets to bear fruit. Outside in the drive, which was a concreted over part of the front garden, was a Rolls Royce, old but clean and tidy. I tried to discuss with the parents the logic of their life. Dad told me, 'life's bloody hard, trying to earn enough money for all this lot. We give the kids so much, and the car and the TV are our only pleasures in life and everyone deserves something good, don't they?' I was at a loss for words, what chance do those little ones have in life I wonder.

I was still pondering that question when I went to another house to deliver a summons. The door was answered by an angelic looking little girl of six or seven years old. 'What the fucking hell do you want?' She said to my astonishment. I stammered out a request to see her dad and she went off shouting, 'Dad, the filth are at the door!'

I came to see that there was an enormous gulf between us, that is between the police and sections of the community. This mutual suspicion, which amounted to something very near hatred, had become a way of life to both sides. If a known villain died, 'good riddance to bad rubbish' was the comment of many of my colleagues. 'If you were lying injured in the gutter I'd spit on yer' was the comment to me of one of the 'enemy'. It became obvious that it was so easy to continue down this route, always suspicious and aggressive to one another, always looking for an opportunity to run down or even harm the other.

It occurred to me that here was an opportunity for me to try to make a difference, to try something new. I parked up my panda car and walked round some of the rough areas. I greeted everyone I met with a smile and a few friendly words. I didn't start too well, I said, 'good morning' to the first man I met. 'Get fucked copper,' came the charming reply! Undaunted, I continued. From then on everyone I met reacted with surprise, and then responded positively. I only met one other surly individual. 'Good morning' I said cheerfully. A cold stare was the only response. 'I'm trying to wish you a good morning my friend'.

'The day a copper is my friend is the day Hell freezes over, so go fuck yourself.' What a lovely fellow! Still two bad responses out of all the people I had spoken to was a pretty good result I felt, showing that stereotypes can be broken down. Of course, a few friendly words are a long way from making responsible citizens who would want to help the police and value their contribution to society, but it was a start.

Chapter 4 Hot Water

I considered myself a generally well-behaved person. I was honest and fair, ok, I cut a few corners but overall I was doing a good job, at least I thought so. Unfortunately, events raised serious doubts about my behaviour during my first year of service.

A colleague, Paul, an experienced senior PC, was responsible for getting me in trouble for the first time. We were sent to a report of a disturbance and arrived to find that there had been an argument between a property owner and his tenant that had descended into fisticuffs. The property owner had a large egg shaped bruise growing nicely on his forehead and was demanding action. Paul knew the guy and having listened to the circumstances told the property owner that he was a shyster getting what he deserved, and as there were no injuries we refused to get involved, he could take out a private summons if he wished. The property owner was furious pointing out, with some justification, that he was injured and fingering the growing lump on his head. Paul replied; 'Well I can't see any lump, can you Jim?' I knew enough to reply hesitantly; 'No, I can't see any lump.'

'Right, I'm going to make an official complaint about you,' asserted our indignant property owner and the following day he did. Unfortunately, he had not taken Paul's number but he had taken mine.

I was soon called in to see the Inspector. Before I went in Paul 'coached' me. 'All quite simple really, it was six of one and half dozen of another, there were NO obvious injuries so we advised him accordingly, right?' 'Err right, Paul' I replied, wishing I could be somewhere else. 'But what if the Inspector has seen the bruise?' 'No problem, it must have grown after we left'.

The Inspector had indeed seen the bruise and wanted to know why I had not taken the proper action, I tried to say convincingly that there was no bruise when I was there. 'Who was the other officer with you?' he demanded. 'It was PC Lord Sir,' 'Ah, PC Lord was it, and I suppose he was the one who did the talking was he?' 'Well yes sir, being the senior man he was showing me the ropes.' 'I hate to think what that man was showing you, tell the Sergeant not to put you out with him again and send PC Lord to see me.' 'Yes, sir' replied a very relieved me as I beat a hasty retreat. PC Lord was duly summoned, duly denied any wrong doing and the complainant was told that his allegation couldn't be substantiated. I didn't like lying, but felt I had little choice. Incidents like that taught me always to try to act correctly, cutting corners and administering our own justice might be very tempting but are dangerous areas to visit.

There was a regular weekly market in town and traffic became a real problem, with congestion particularly intense on the approaches to the market.

I was out on patrol with Mike when we were directed to the market to try and help with traffic. We stood in the road and tried to sort it out. Another call came in and Mike decided to leave me there while he attended, promising to return as soon as he could. Because of the congestion, traffic was tailing back onto the main road. To overcome this we stopped vehicles from taking their usual route into the market, sending them on a more circuitous route.

One motorist was very upset at my directions. He left his car blocking the road and got out to remonstrate with me. 'You're causing more trouble than good, get out of the way and let me into the market.' 'The number of vehicles trying to go in is tailing back onto the main road and blocking up the town, I'm afraid you will have to go round.' 'This is ridiculous, the queue's not into the main road now, so why don't you be a good lad and get out of the way.' There's no queue because of my actions, now go round like everyone else.' 'How old are you? They've sent out a boy to do a man's job and you're making a pig's ear of it.' 'Look, I've asked you nicely. Now I'm telling you, get back into your car and drive round.' 'Bloody jumped up little Hitler aren't you, no brains, just pig ignorant.' 'That's enough, if you don't piss off this minute I'm going to nick you.' 'You can't talk to me like that, I'm going, but you haven't heard the last of this!'

I shouldn't have spoken to him like that, but well, what did he expect? Mike returned and all went smoothly enough as the volume of traffic gradually subsided. An hour or so later I was called back to the Station to see the Inspector, oh heck! 'I've just had a complaint about you, PC Cannon, that you were unnecessarily obstructive to a member of the public and then swore at him?' 'It wasn't like that at all Sir.' I went on to explain what had happened, substituting 'clear off' for 'piss off', well it was only a little lie! 'I've tried to talk him out of it, but he is insistent that he wants to make an official complaint.' 'What does that mean, sir?' 'It means that an investigating officer will be appointed and you will be served with papers, explaining the procedure. I am a little concerned that you've only been in the job five minutes and this is your second complaint.' 'I don't know what to say Sir; I was only trying to do my job.' 'Well, we will see what happens, get back on patrol and for God's sake be careful about what you do and say.'

Within a few days, I was summoned to return to the Station to meet with a Superintendent, the investigating officer for the complaint. I duly presented myself and was served with papers outlining the complaint and warning me of the possible consequences if the allegation was substantiated. Senior colleagues had advised me to refuse to co-operate and say nothing. I didn't intend to follow that advice, because apart from my little indiscretion of language I felt I was in the right. It made sense to state my case and try to avoid going before the Chief Constable in a full Disciplinary Hearing. I therefore explained my side of the story to the Superintendent. He brought up the previous complaint. I pointed out that it was unfair to include that as it involved a much more senior PC and the allegation had been dismissed. He prevailed on me to make a statement, which I did, and he went off to process the matter.

I was very worried about it, because as a probationer I was extremely vulnerable. I could be dismissed at any time, and didn't have the rights of a substantive PC. Time dragged by and then I was summoned to Divisional Headquarters to see the Chief Superintendent. He was a dour, humourless Scotsman, and I didn't think mercy and understanding would be high on his list of attributes. Shaking in my boots, I went in to see him. He went through the allegation all over again and I had to explain all over again. Finally, he said that his view and that of the Investigating Officer was that the complaint was unproven. In the circumstances, they intended to record a Divisional Reprimand on my record, but there would be no formal discipline proceedings. I didn't know whether to be angry or pleased. I tried to argue my case but got nowhere. I was sent back to the Station after being warned as to my future conduct.

Reflecting on the complaint, I was angry about it. Surely, supervisors should trust their officers and refuse to proceed in unsubstantiated and vigorously denied allegations. I suppose they went on the 'no smoke without fire' principle. At any event, there was no point worrying about it; I must just make sure that I keep out of trouble. As the Chief Superintendent pointed out, most officers go through their entire service without having a complaint against them, whereas I had been complained about twice within a few months.

I managed to avoid a complaint for the next few months but it was not to last. One afternoon I was called to the scene of a road traffic accident. One vehicle seemed to have lost control and collided with an oncoming vehicle. Damage was extensive but there only seemed to be minor injuries. The usual crowd of people were there and it took me a while to realise that the driver of the offending vehicle was not there. Enquiries revealed that he had been seen running off towards a nearby estate. I obtained a good description and went off to look for him, leaving other officers to sort out the scene.

It wasn't long before I saw a man matching his description at the far edge of the estate. I got out of the car, approached him and called on him to stop. He made out that he didn't hear me and continued until I caught up with him and physically restrained him. He protested vigorously and denied being in the car or knowing anything about it. He had minor bumps and abrasions consistent with an accident and he fitted the description very well. I therefore told him that I believed he was the driver and as I could smell alcohol, I required a breath test. He refused, continuing to deny any involvement. I arrested him, but he didn't come quietly and I had to get some help to subdue him, get him into a police car and back to the Station.

At the Station, he continued to struggle, shout, and swear at me as I took him into the charge room. I explained what had happened to the Sergeant and as I did so, the duty Inspector came along to see what all the fuss was about. At the sight of the Inspector the man calmed down somewhat and asked to make a complaint. The Inspector told him he would take his complaint after I had dealt with him. He took me outside and told me to make sure everything was done by the book and not to allow him to provoke me in any way. I assured him that I would remain calm and returned to the room to continue the procedure.

After a while, things seemed calmer, so the Sergeant left me to it, although he promised to remain within hearing range. As soon as he was gone, the man went back to threatening me, saying he would find out where I lived and he and his mates would come and get me. This was the first time I had been threatened like this and I didn't like it, but I remained calm and carried on. I was standing up, bending over the table writing, he was sitting on a chair at the edge of the table. Suddenly he reached into my long truncheon pocket and pulled my truncheon out! I reacted quickly, I didn't want to be hit with my own truncheon or embarrassed by colleagues seeing my situation. I leapt on him as he stood up and a violent struggle ensued, he was bigger than I was but my momentum forced him backwards as I held his wrist. I heard running footsteps as people came to see what all the noise was about. With a supreme effort, I pushed him backwards and wrested the truncheon from his grasp. He fell backwards, there was a large bin there, the size of a dustbin, and he fell into it, doubled up and stuck there!

That was the scene as the Sergeant and Inspector came into the room. The Inspector took one look and said, 'come outside Cannon, I want a word with you. I thought I told you to go by the book and keep calm'. 'Well, yes sir, but I had no choice.' 'What do you mean, you had no choice?' Reluctantly and sheepishly, I explained what had happened while I looked through the open door watching the Sergeant extract my prisoner from the waste bin, trying hard not to laugh as he did so. 'I hope you will be more careful in future and that you've learned an important lesson.' 'Yes, sir' I replied, and I had, always keep any actual or potential weapons out of reach, especially if dealing with a violent prisoner.

I hoped that would be the end of it, but the offender insisted on registering his complaint with the Inspector. My heart sank; I was really in trouble this time! An investigating officer was duly appointed, papers were served on me and the process began again. This time it was alleged that I had made a false arrest, been unnecessarily violent, rude and abusive. The complainant intended to call the Sergeant and Inspector as witnesses. My first thought was that they would surely support my version of events. Then I realised that all they had actually seen was the man in the dustbin, the rest of their knowledge came from my account. Things looked very bleak indeed. The investigating Superintendent gave me a hard time in the interview and I got the distinct impression that he didn't believe me. I declined to make another written statement and suggested he used the one I had provided for the complainants prosecution, and told him that I stood by every word.

Over the next few weeks, the Sergeant and Inspector were interviewed. They were not allowed to tell me anything they had said, and I was really nervous and stressed about it all. Eventually I was called up to see the Chief Superintendent, a different one from last time, and seemingly more approachable.

'Come in PC Cannon and sit down.' 'Yes, sir.' 'You're a bloody disgrace Cannon, beating up members of the public, swearing and abusing people and failing to do your duty. Three complaints in some six months! What have you got to say for yourself?' I was shocked by this attack and took a moment to gather my thoughts. 'I have done nothing wrong; in each case I did what I believed was right. I know I made a mistake in letting this complainant get my truncheon, but surely you see that I had to retrieve it quickly and vigorously. He was violent, aggressive and threatening throughout, while I simply did my job as well as I can.' He looked at me for a few moments and then a big smile spread across his face. 'Of course you did, I'm completely satisfied that, apart from losing your truncheon, you acted correctly and bravely. Any police officer who is really doing his job, getting involved with people as he should, will attract complaints and it's my view that the odd complaint shows that you are doing what you're paid for.' What a relief! 'I've marked the file, `malicious complaint`; there will be no further action against you. We have to investigate these things, but I believe you're doing a good job so go back to your Station and carry on the good work.'

There was a spring in my step and a great weight lifted off my shoulders as I returned to work, encouraged and fired up to do my best. I was complained about several more times during my service, thankfully after I had completed my probationary two years. None of the complaints ever led to my appearance before a Disciplinary Tribunal.

One of those complaints involved the property owner I first clashed with when patrolling with Paul. On this occasion, I attended the report of a theft in another part of town. Waiting for me was my friend the property owner and two women. He had been collecting rents at some of his properties when he saw two women stealing his property. It was just before Christmas and the girls had spotted some holly on an overgrown tree in the front garden of one of his properties. They broke a couple of branches off. A dastardly act that in his view deserved the full weight of the law being brought to bear. He had carried out a citizen's arrest of the two poor women.

I couldn't believe my ears, the tree or bush was completely uncultivated in an untended and overgrown front garden. Aware that a complaint hung in the air, I nevertheless wasn't going to comply with his request. He demanded that I take the women into custody under arrest, and take them to court as he wished to support a prosecution. I told him that in my view it was a trivial and inconsequential matter, about which I intended to take no action, beyond releasing the women. If he really wanted the holly back, he could have it. Our conversation continued something like this, 'theft is theft. I have caught these women stealing my property and I demand that you do your duty and take them in.' 'In view of the state of this holly bush, and the property in general, these women made the assumption that the holly was there for the taking. As far as I'm concerned there is no criminal intent and I am not going to take any action.' 'I remember you; you refused to do your duty when I got hit by a tenant.' 'That's not the matter at issue. You have made an allegation and I am not prepared to act on it.'

There was a lengthy pause; I began to hope for a positive outcome. Then he piped up again, 'I complained about you last time and I'm going to complain about you this time. You've obviously got it in for me, you haven't done your duty and you're a bloody disgrace.' Aware of my temper rising, I replied, 'and you're a pain in the neck, you're a mean spirited miserable individual who gives human kindness a bad name.' To the women, 'you're free to go, forget all about this rubbish, and I wish you a happy Christmas.' Turning back to the man, 'I suggest you buy a copy of "A Christmas Carol" There's a bloke in there who's nearly as bad as you, see what happened to him. Now stop wasting police time and try and learn some kindness.' I left him still shouting after me complaining about injustice.

Sure enough, he made a complaint. The Inspector who took the complaint couldn't believe it either. I had the women's details in case I needed witnesses, but the complaint was dismissed out of hand, and a report to that effect was filed.

Despite the decisive response to that complaint, it was a source of irritation that much of the public and the press believed that the police didn't investigate their own. My experience was that they vigorously investigated their own, and were more likely to prosecute a police officer than a member of the public. If a police officer was involved in a road accident with a member of the public, the member of the public was very unlikely to be prosecuted. Not so the police officer. At the political level in the police force senior officers were determined to try to ensure that the police looked whiter than white. One can't blame them for that, but that concern was in danger of taking priority over everything else, perhaps even justice. At my level, it caused considerable dissatisfaction to know that some senior officers were more concerned about the public image of the police rather than the rights and wrongs of a particular case, and were therefore unlikely to back us if we got into trouble.

Chapter 5 Colleagues

Public support is very important for an effective police service. I would go as far as to say that without public support the police are rendered largely ineffective. Public-spirited members of the public are the eyes and ears of the police, and those who have had a bad experience are unlikely to help in any way. Courtesy costs nothing and it is so important for officers to put themselves in the shoes of whomever they are dealing with. An experienced officer may have dealt with hundreds of burglaries and for him they are just routine, but the person he is dealing with is probably experiencing burglary for the first time and having a rare contact with the police. Treating it as all very routine and boring is really disrespectful, and is quite likely to cause ill feeling against the police. It costs nothing to treat them and their crime seriously and it generates a good deal of goodwill. Similarly, an errant motorist doesn't have to be made a fool of, especially in front of others, and if they need to be reported for an offence, it can be done politely.

When a member of the public is unfairly treated, it is not just them who are upset. They will relate the incident to their family and friends, who will in turn pass it on to their circle, and the story will grow in the telling. Their negative view of the police will inevitably colour the judgement of their family and friends. In the same way, a positive encounter will be shared with many others.

Since I have left the police, I have come into contact with police officers in a number of ways. Sometimes they were fine, but on other occasions they looked so bored and disinterested in what I had to say, and did little more than go through the motions. I'm certainly not claiming that I was perfect, far from it. I'm quite sure that there were times when I was offhand and abrupt, but if I realised later I always regretted it and tried not to do it. As I became more experienced and could exert some influence on new recruits or colleagues, I tried to encourage them to seek to be polite in all circumstances.

I was sometimes quite shocked by the attitude of some of the senior Constables. On one occasion, I was with a senior man in a police car when we were sent to deliver a death message. For most officers this is one of our most onerous duties. In this case, just before Christmas, we had to tell a woman that her husband, a man in his early 50's, had collapsed and died at work on the night shift.

We turned up at his home early in the morning. The house was all ready for Christmas, the Christmas tree was up, presents lay under it, and the decorations and cards were in place. On the mantelpiece above the fireplace were what looked like the husband's glasses. As gently as I could, I broke the news to the lady of the house. She reacted quite violently and began beating my chest screaming, 'it's not true, it's not true'. I tried to calm her down and my colleague offered the helpful, 'for God's sake pull yourself together woman'. Eventually she did calm down and I made her a cup of tea while my colleague fretted about getting back on patrol. We contacted her family, waited until they had arrived and left her in their care. As we walked down the drive my colleague's comment was, 'stupid cow.' I think we spent most of the rest of the shift arguing about his attitude, but I realised that his reaction was the way he coped, closing down feelings to avoid any hurt.

I was with the same officer one evening in the rural area when we stopped a transit van containing a number of members of the traveller's fraternity, gypsies to most of us. They gave us a bit of lip, which is quite usual, and my colleague responded; 'I hate you bloody pikies!' A very tense standoff resulted which could easily have descended into violence. Fortunately, it didn't and we lived to fight another day. Another interesting conversation between us followed. Give him his due, he feared no one and spoke in the same way to everyone. We stopped a chauffeur driven Rolls Royce one day and in the back was a well-dressed man of mature years. Next to him was a glamorous young blonde-haired woman. 'I suppose you're going to tell me this is your wife,' said my tactful friend.

My colleagues were a very interesting bunch. I learned much from them and saw a few things that I would not want to adopt as my practice. There were a number of men who had seen service in the Second World War and then joined up. These men all had well over 20 years of service and would be retiring over the next few years. They belonged to the days when a good clip round the ear was standard practice, when there were no breath tests - I don't ever remember an officer of their service arresting someone for failing a breath test - few cars and no radio, which made doing their own thing rather easier than it is today. Some had become very cynical over the years.

One in particular was a man not to cross. A famous story of him was told where he was in a police car responding to a call to trouble at the cinema. He was notorious for taking his time and when he arrived, the incident was over and a plain-clothes officer was sitting on the bonnet of a police car while other officers were inside the cinema taking details having dealt with the problem. Our hero leapt out of his car, drew his truncheon and started beating the plain-clothes officer about the head. Other officers pulled him off pointing out that he was one of us. 'Shouldn't have such bloody long hair then' was our friends only comment!

This wasn't the first such incident and to avoid further problems he was moved to jailer duties inside the Station. That should have provided maximum supervision and therefore no more incidents. That's what they thought! He had a special rubber truncheon made, because it left fewer marks, and woe betide any prisoner who crossed him. I first realised this officer's effect on people when I accompanied him on a prisoner run to a nearby Prison. We had a driver and five prisoners, some very hard looking men among them. They had all been in the tender care of my colleague since their arrest. As we drove on, he suddenly barked, 'smoke' and immediately five hands proffered cigarettes to him. Amazing! I was told he was frightened of his wife but I have no evidence to support that!

I was in the Station one day and there was a prisoner in the cells shouting insults and curses at all and sundry. Our friendly jailer tried to quieten him with verbal threats to no avail. He then flattened himself against the wall and crept up on the man whose head was protruding from the cell flap to add more volume to his shouting. Our jailer grabbed him by the hair, pulled his head out of the flap into the corridor and proceeded to beat him about the head with his truncheon! He literally foamed at the mouth with effort and anger. Other officers rushed to stop him before he did really serious damage. He did stop, briefly, and then hit him a couple more times before slamming the cell flap against his head catapulting him back into the cell. Thankfully, the prisoner wasn't seriously hurt, he didn't complain and surprise, surprise, he was no further trouble during his period in custody.

The same officer was walking through the Police Station passing an interview room when he overheard a man refusing to tell an officer his name and address. In he went, a belt round the ear followed, 'now tell the officer,' he said. He was hustled outside where it was pointed out that the man he had just struck was simply a witness!

Fortunately unknown by senior officers, he took his lunch in a local brewery. The people at the brewery complained to us about him. Apparently, he sat next to the beer barrel, said nothing to anyone else, and simply drank as much as he could in the 45 minutes he had available. They said that he drank up to 12 pints of beer! That seemed to me an astonishing amount in so short a time, but even allowing a 50% exaggeration it was still a great deal of beer. Perhaps it's not surprising that some of his worst excesses happened after lunch!

Things finally came to a head when he was taking two prisoners from the Station to appear in court, which was just across the police yard. The two men were handcuffed together and as they crossed the yard they made a break for freedom. They broke free from the jailer, ran out into the street, and down towards the town centre, hotly pursued by our hero yelling dire threats. It was market day and the street was very busy with cars and pedestrians. The two prisoners had to dodge in and out of people and as they did, they ran either side of a lamppost! That brought them up with a start. You can probably guess what happened next. The jailer caught up with them, drew his truncheon and began administering his form of 'justice' as he muttered; 'I'll teach you to try and escape from me.'

It was decided to move him to a yet safer place and he was sent to the Crown Court to make sure there were no problems there. All seemed well for some time until one day when I was on duty in the Station. A man came in with his nose battered and bleeding. 'I want to make a complaint,' he said.

I asked him what had happened and he said, 'well I was at the Crown Court where my son was on trial. He was found guilty and the Judge sentenced him to three years and, well I got a bit upset and shouted at the Judge. He told the Policeman there to put me out of the court. I suppose that was fair enough, but as soon as the Judge couldn't see he punched me on the nose!' I got an Inspector to take the complaint but the complainant didn't want a prosecution, just a warning, so he got away with it again.

The last brush he had with officialdom came when every officer was needed to police a march, comprised mostly of women protesting about the need for a pedestrian crossing on a part of a road where one of their children had recently been killed. The Superintendent placed our hero at a strategic point and told him not to let anyone pass him. The march deviated from their scheduled route and turned towards the man of the hour. The leaders of the march approached him. He told them that they couldn't pass but they were having none of it and went to go by. The nearest mother was immediately grabbed by the throat, shaken around a bit and then thrown to the ground! They did not pass. There was a considerable fuss and the press were involved. Next day the local paper put the story on the front page under the banner headline of something on the lines of 'Police Brutality at peaceful march.' When questioned about the incident the officer replied, 'I can't see what all the fuss is about, the Superintendent told me that no one was to pass and no one did'. How he got away with such things was beyond me, but he managed to complete his 30 years and retire on a full pension.

A certain Detective Inspector was fond of a drink, and during the lunchtime at a Crown Court trial, he had a few before resuming his seat behind counsel at the front of the court. The defendant took the witness box and was asked his name and then his occupation. At that point, a very loud whisper was heard from behind counsel, 'he's a fucking thief'. Apparently, the Judge was far from amused! The same man took his truncheon, drilled out the centre and filled it with lead. The opportunity arose to put it to the test when he attended a violent confrontation. He approached a large black man who was fighting furiously and struck him forcefully on the back of the head with his heavy truncheon. The man turned and looked at him, 'don't you ever do that again', he said to the astonished Inspector!

Then there was Steve. He was one of those people who exude super confidence; always have an answer for everything and whose education seemed to include detailed knowledge of every subject under the sun. He did have a degree in some obscure engineering subject. His common sense sometimes left something to be desired. In one famous incident, he commandeered a milk float to chase a stolen car. No, he didn't catch it! He had his leg pulled by the others about this and his wide 'knowledge', and usually seemed not to notice. One day we were in the canteen and he had been pontificating about something or other and then fell asleep with his bald head lying on his arms on the table. In front of him was his half-drunk cup of tea, now cold. We carefully balanced the cup on his bald pate, crept out of the door and then slammed it shut. We went along the corridor laughing as, 'you bastards' echoed through the door!

One of the senior men on the section was Sean. He was a natural thief-taker and made more arrests than anyone else. He seemed to have the ability to sense when someone had something to hide and would pull people in with no evidence, and Sean had no idea of what, or even if, they had done anything. He would interview them skilfully, gradually extracting information and almost invariably, they admitted something before long. His other claim to fame was his ability to consume alcohol. He had been known to consume a good skin-full, go into the loo, throw up and then return to the bar and carry on drinking! Nevertheless, he was a good man to have around and I tried to learn from him. I have to admit I never managed to develop the coppers nose he had. Perhaps inevitably he went on to have a successful career in C.I.D.

I've mentioned Paul before, the officer who got me my first complaint and who I wasn't allowed to go out with again, certainly until I was more experienced. He was likeable enough and perfectly capable, but he could be lazy and was very cynical. He had little time for senior officers, especially if they had 'no bottle' i.e. no courage in difficult situations. We were sitting at parade one evening preparing for our shift, when the Inspector came in. We all stood up as we were expected to in the presence of a senior officer. That is we all stood up except Paul, who didn't move. 'Don't you stand up for an Inspector PC Lord?' Asked the Inspector. 'Only if I respect him,' replied Paul, 'and I don't respect you.' There was a stunned silence before the red faced Inspector told us all to sit down. I never knew what history they had between them but the Inspector took no action despite the serious loss of face and potential undermining of discipline.

On another occasion, there was a call to trouble in a pub. The attending officers shouted for help and we all dropped everything and went to help them. A Sergeant, other than our own, was working with us that day, and was out on patrol in one of the cars. When the call went out, he told the driver to drop him off before the PC attended the incident. The incident was duly dealt with and order was restored. We all noticed the Sergeant's absence at the scene, and the PC who was with him told us what had happened. At the end of our shift, we returned to the Station. The Sergeant was waiting for us, and congratulated us on dealing with the incident so effectively. In front of us all Paul said, 'no thanks to you, you are a fucking useless Sergeant'. The Sergeant blushed but said nothing, what could he say, he had lost the respect of all of us. Strange, because he stood well over six feet tall and was very powerfully built, being a weight lifting instructor! Size and strength had little to do with 'bottle'.

Our own Sergeant certainly didn't suffer from 'lack of bottle.' From the time I first met him, he was always immaculately turned out, uniform creased in all the right places, boots bulled to a real shine, hair short and neat and of course his wonderful handlebar moustache trimmed and waxed. He had seen service in the war in the army and was very much of the old school. He was fair, had a great sense of humour and led from the front. If there was trouble, he would face it head on and was an inspiration to us.

Shortly before I joined, he had been involved in a major incident with a large number of gypsies at their encampment. Something like 27 officers required hospital treatment and a large amount of police equipment, from cars on downwards, had been damaged. The police had gone to the site in some force to arrest a number of men who had long been suspected of a series of crimes across the area. The men had a record of violence, especially against police, but no raid was planned at that time. However, matters were brought to a head by an incident involving two officers in a patrol car who pursued a suspect vehicle onto the site. Men emerged from caravans and launched a vicious attack on the two officers. Not content with attacking them their police vehicle was almost completely destroyed.

They had called for assistance and other cars arrived and took them away from danger. The Duty Inspector than gathered as many men as he could and returned to the site, the original officers knew which gypsies had attacked them, so the Inspector knocked on the door of their caravan and demanded that the four brothers believed responsible should come out. One of the brothers was on crutches. He came to the door, swung his crutch, the Inspector ducked and the officer behind had his jaw broken. A missile was thrown from the caravan inflicting serious facial injuries on another officer; there was a warning klaxon on the site, which the travellers used for just such an eventuality. This was sounded and a crowd of gypsies emerged and the incident exploded into a major and violent confrontation

The case eventually came to Crown Court and the defence was that these `poor innocent` gypsy men had been set upon by a large number of violent Policemen. Sergeant Frank gave his evidence, and then one of the defence barristers stood to cross-examine. That cross-examination went something like this. 'Sergeant, can you tell me the rules regarding the use of police truncheons?' Frank explained that they should only be used in situations of extreme violence and then offenders should be struck on the arms or legs, not the head. 'Thank you Sergeant. Now I put it to you that you deliberately disobeyed those rules and struck my client on the head with your truncheon?' 'Yes sir.' 'I further put it to you that you struck my client with great force?' 'Yes sir.' 'And I further suggest that you struck my client not just once but several times?' 'Yes sir.' By this time, the barrister was almost rubbing his hands together with glee. Frank then turned to the judge and asked if he could explain, and despite the barristers objections he was duly given permission. 'I have been a Policeman for 24 years, during that time I have been involved in a large number of violent situations. Before I joined the police, I served with the army and fought for my country in the last war. In all that time, I have been in a number of violent and dangerous situations. That night on the gypsy site was as violent and dangerous a situation, if not more so than any other I have faced. A number of officers had been injured and a great deal of equipment damaged. The defendants and their compatriots were throwing heavy missiles from a caravan at officers who had tried to get into the caravan and had been beaten back with serious injuries. Other officers were involved in desperate fighting with a large number of gypsies armed with all sorts of weapons. I was close to the caravan and every time a head poked out of a window I hit it with all the force I could muster!' The defence barrister sat down deflated and defeated.

What a superb example that was too all of us young officers. Tell the truth, explain why you did what you did and don't be frightened to ask for permission to explain when a barrister is deliberately trying to lead you down a path that will not reveal the full truth. It was a lesson I never forgot and have used very successfully on a number of occasions.

Another of my colleagues who was a real character was Roy, he was blessed with a good dose of earthy common sense, which I respected although some of the senior officers didn't. He stopped a car one day and saw that one of the tyres was bald. Instead of reporting the owner for summons, he checked his spare, which was okay, and made him change the tyre then and there. I call that good common sense.

On another occasion, he was called to a report of youths causing trouble. A group of youths were misbehaving opposite a queue of people at a bus stop. Roy made them all turn their pockets out and lay their belongings on the window ledge of a nearby shop. Then he mixed up all their belongings and swept them on to the ground. As the youths bent over to pick them up, he gave each one a sharp kick in the rear. The people in the bus queue thought it was wonderful and burst into spontaneous applause as the youths slunk away, humiliated. A technique definitely not in the police manual but very effective!

He and a colleague were cornered one day by four large and very hostile gypsies who were intent on giving them a good beating. Roy said to them, 'I don't doubt that you will win, but it'll cost you cos we'll hurt you bad and we'll remember your faces and one day or one dark night we'll meet again when there's more of us than you and you'll get the hiding of your lives.' Maybe it was just a bluff but it worked, and his colleague related the story to us with obvious and heartfelt relief!

Roy decided to join a few of us who were weight training after work one afternoon. He watched for a while until we were lying on our backs lifting a 56lb weight with each hand, bringing them up in an arc from our sides to meet above our heads. He decided he wanted a go. We pointed out that if he hadn't done it before he would be wise to start with a lighter weight. He wouldn't hear of it. 'If you can do it, I can do it.' So he lay on the bench, grasped the two heavy weights and commenced the arc. He was right handed, and with considerable effort, the weight in his right hand came up to its correct position above his head. The left was obviously much tougher, eventually with much strain and grunting, his arm quivering with the effort the weight neared the vertical position. Unfortunately, he couldn't quite make it and his strength gave out, the weight falling onto his head! I think it must have knocked some sense into him because he never joined us for weight lifting again.

I can't leave colleagues without mentioning Rob. He was young and strong with a pretty short fuse and prepared to take chances. Like many of us, he had trouble with local youths but they picked the wrong man with him. One day in a busy town centre road, he was confronted by a group of youths. He decided to arrest the leader for public order offences. The youth wasn't going to come quietly and he stood a good head taller than Rob did. Violence looked imminent; Rob remained calm and then seemingly quite casually removed his helmet, as if to wipe his forehead. Then he suddenly head butted the guy, catching him squarely on the jaw. He went down like a sack of potatoes and was no further trouble. Rob calmly replaced his helmet and radioed in for a car to come and collect his prisoner! He certainly had style, and as time went on, he proved himself fearless and a good man to have by your side in trouble.

As well as all the characters there were other men, much quieter perhaps, but good workers, men you could rely on in a tight corner, and who on the whole were a credit to the police service. The two men who regularly crewed the emergency vehicle, a Ford Escort Estate, were both excellent police officers, always responding promptly to calls and bringing in a steady stream of good quality arrests. Some of these men became very good friends of mine and we are still in touch over 30 years later. There were no women among them, because in those days there were no women on section shift work. There was a WPC Unit, with some very capable women, but their work was generally confined to children, battered wives, sexual offences, Station duties etc.

Chapter 6 Ongoing Training

Around the time I joined, there were several other recruits. New Constables are on probation for two years with regular evaluations until, hopefully, their appointment is confirmed. Inevitably perhaps, not all made it. One keen and likeable young man just could not do his paperwork and was seriously disorganised, we wanted to help him and did what we could but he went after just a few months.

Then there was young Dave. He was very slightly built and although keen and brave enough, tended to be picked upon in confrontational situations. He was driving to work for nights one evening when he came across a fight in the street. He pulled alongside the participants, introduced himself as a police officer and told them to stop. One of them turned to him and hit him in the face, breaking his nose. On another occasion, Paul had to rescue him from a pub disturbance when a big angry customer had him by the lapels and lifted him right off his feet! He was picked on by the town youths and one large and well-known troublemaker cornered him in a shop doorway one night, threatening violence. Dave hit him over the head with his big three-cell torch and the man had the cheek to come and complain. He was given short shrift.

After a few incidents like this serious discussions went on, he had other problems of punctuality and paperwork and it was mutually agreed that perhaps Dave wasn't cut out for the life of a police officer. We were sorry to see him go as we were for all those who didn't make it. They had become friends and colleagues and senior men had tried to help them through. The camaraderie that developed between most of us was a very special thing, we had to rely on one another, sometimes in very difficult situations, and a very real bond can develop, a friend in need is a friend indeed as the old saying goes.

As had been my experience related in chapter 1, initial Training consisted of one residential week at Headquarters, 13 weeks away at a Regional Training Centre and then 2 more residential weeks at Headquarters. Following that were six weeks on patrol accompanied by a tutor Constable. If that all went well, an officer could patrol alone. Monthly attendance for one days training was obligatory for the two years of probation, and after about 18 months, there was a four-week residential continuation course. An evaluation was made every three months and some time around 21 months the final decision was made. If there were problems but also promise shown, it was possible for the probationary period to be extended for up to a year. How you were getting on was a constant source of concern, as were the different ways of being evaluated. The Sergeant's were all different. Some of them judged officers on how many arrests you made, some on how many people you reported for summons - which required some persecution of motorists, and others looked at your general work rate and paid little attention to statistics. I soon learned to work out which was which.

Not surprisingly, old school Sergeants made a general evaluation, ex traffic Sergeants wanted lots of offences reported and ex - CID Sergeants were likely to judge your arrests. I had no complaint about their fairness but I was aware of this difference in perception.

After one of my early evaluations, I was called up to see the Superintendent. I had been to see him once before when I first reported at the Station and I had lived to tell the tale! He was a great big man, ex-CID, very prone to shouting and swearing and he was universally feared. He enjoyed the fear he engendered, and give him his due; he admired the few men who stood up to him. Upstairs I went to his office, knocked, entered, and gave him my smartest salute. 'Sit down', he ordered and I took my helmet off and sat opposite him across the desk. Then he just looked at me. He said nothing just glared at me with a penetrating stare. I was only slightly trembling in my boots but I tried hard not to show it. I knew my report was good so I should have nothing to worry about. Of course, as the stare continued and the silence grew increasingly oppressive I began to doubt myself, what had I done, what did he know? Eventually he said, 'you look rather uncomfortable my old cocker, what have you got to tell me?' I later learned that this was one of his techniques for getting a confession, a 'cough' as it's known in the trade. I replied that I had nothing to tell him, 'you sure son? Better to get it off your chest, I know lots go on that you lads think I don't know about, but I'm not daft you know.' I assured him that not for the tiniest weeniest infinitesimal fraction of a second did I think he was daft but I still had nothing to tell him! After another prolonged stare, he switched from this line of questioning and went on to discuss my progress report. The rest of the interview went well and he concluded by telling me to keep up the good work. Very relieved, I tried to take my time as I replaced my helmet and saluted smartly before I retired to the lower reaches of the Station to recover from the experience.

Monthly training days were held at Downchester Police Station, a six-storey glass building with good views over the River Downs and the City of Downchester. To be honest I can remember little of the substance of those training days. I usually found them dull and uninspiring and would much rather have been out on patrol. The only good things about the day were the meals in their canteen on the top floor. At Brightstone, we had limited cooking facilities available for our use. At Downchester, they had excellent facilities in a fully equipped kitchen and a full-time cook and assistant cook, and they were good at their job. .

Another part of training was attachments to various specialist units, particularly CID and Traffic. My two-week traffic attachment was something I didn't much look forward to. I had learned during initial training that the minutiae of Road Traffic Law bored me to tears, and I knew that I didn't know it well enough to venture to stop a heavy goods vehicle, or HGV, and check it over. I was soon on patrol in a powerful traffic car; at that time they were Rover 3500's which were very rapid indeed and very comfortable. I tried to look interested when my colleague enthused about something wrong with a close coupled trailer, or when he stopped an overweight vehicle because he was able to detect it was overweight by the way it sat on the axles, or when an HGV driver had gone over his allotted hours, whatever they were! The police cars were equipped with a device called VASCAR, which aided them in detecting a speeding vehicle from a considerable distance. Most motorists do speed I guess and when we drove along a considerable length of a major trunk road at exactly 70 mph, there was a very long queue behind us, together with a number of worried motorists who had been speeding along overtaking in the outside lane before they suddenly saw us and had to brake sharply. My colleague enjoyed the power and influence he had, but I doubt if members of the public enjoyed the experience.

Most traffic officers prided themselves on the quality of their driving and believed in their ability to control driving situations in a way beyond ordinary mortals. I readily admit that some of them were superb drivers and made me feel reasonably safe, even at high speeds. One of them got into a discussion about driving with a garage owner who was involved in stock car racing. He challenged the traffic man to join in a race. He agreed, took part in the race and duly won!

A good proportion of traffic men showed little mercy to offenders. As one said to me, 'if they're stupid enough to commit an offence I'm stupid enough to book them for it'. Not a philosophy I would share. Of course, not all were like that and I got on fine with many of them. Some of them had interesting ways of patrolling their area. One officer was particularly interested in young women and knew all the places where he would get the best view of numbers of girls going to work, coming off the train and even getting changed with the curtains open. I had to put up with this although of course I had no interest in the girls at all! Others liked their tea and had developed a good number of tea stops around their area, where we seemed to spend an inordinate amount of time. The majority worked hard enough and did a job I wouldn't want to do.

It was during my traffic attachment that I attended my first fatal road traffic accident. We were on the motorway when the call came over the radio asking us to attend an accident and we sped off, lights and horns blazing and travelling at well over 100 mph, an exhilarating experience actually. We were the first vehicle on the scene of the accident, which was just off the motorway in the nearside lane of a fast section of dual carriageway.

My colleague leapt out of the car to place cones and make sure the scene was safe from passing traffic, leaving me to go to those involved. By the side of the road was a car so badly damaged that it was impossible to determine what make it was. Another car was in front of it undamaged, and in the nearside lane was a 32-ton HGV. In the road next to the damaged car was a young man lying in an ever-increasing pool of blood. As I approached, I could see that he had sustained a terrible head injury with a hole in his head exposing his brain. A deep laceration extended across his face from cheekbone to jaw, right across his lips. His trousers were ripped apart and the calf muscle of one leg was hanging on by just a small flap of skin. His pelvic area was obviously extensively damaged.

Amazingly, he was still alive although unconscious, and his breath came in short frothy blood stained gasps. I stood there in horror, what on earth could I do for him? I eased his head and put a blanket under him as his breathing slowed and death neared. I had been trained in First Aid but I didn't know where to start and the horror of the situation didn't help my thinking.

As I stood there a passing car stopped and a woman approached me, she explained that she was a nurse and could she help. I was obscuring the injured man until she was quite close. As she came near she saw the man, 'oh you poor man' and she was there, checking his pulse and then giving him oral resuscitation, the kiss of life, right across those torn and bleeding lips. I watched in amazement, overwhelmed by the compassion and care of this nurse and my own helplessness. Before too long an ambulance arrived and the crew took over from the nurse. She got back into her car and drove on, I never saw her again and never had the chance to thank her for her gallant efforts. After working on him for a while, the ambulance men put him on a stretcher and into the ambulance. I went with them, as one of the crew continued his efforts to save the injured man's life. It was a hopeless task and he died as we drove to the hospital. The ambulance man fought on for a while before being forced to accept the inevitable. When we arrived at the Hospital, a doctor came out and certified death and he was taken straight to the Mortuary. They had to tip the pool of blood off the stretcher before it could go for cleaning.

My colleague was busy taking statements and undertaking the harrowing job of notifying relatives, so it was some time before we met up and I was able to discover what had happened. Apparently, the dead man had stopped his car and pulled onto the grass verge after his windscreen shattered. Another motorist saw the problem and stopped in front of him to see if he could help. As they were talking by the car, the 32-ton HGV came along the road. Either there was a sudden serious mechanical breakdown or, more likely, the driver nodded off, at any event, the HGV left the road, struck the driver in the head causing terrible injuries and knocking him into the carriageway. The HGV then went right over his car crushing it completely. The driver, perhaps shaken into wakefulness, then pulled back onto the road and as he did so, he ran over the injured man causing those awful leg and pelvic injuries. A moment's inattention with such terrible consequences. The driver of the HGV was obviously very shocked but uninjured. He had been reported for summons for causing death by dangerous driving and a full report would be prepared. I was told that as I had dealt with the dead man I was to attend his post mortem examination the following morning.

I went home that afternoon quite traumatised by the accident. Too often police officers acted as if they exist in a macho culture where they could see or deal with anything and then shrug it off. It wasn't true for most of them and it certainly wasn't true for me. Many officers became deliberately hardened to tragedy as their way of coping. I feared that doing that meant losing part of one's humanity. Much better to enter into the tragedy, empathise as much as possible, but still be able to do the job. That hurt more and took more out of you, but it was human and real. I was deeply affected by the horror of the accident, my inability to do anything to help, the example of the nurse, watching a man die for the first time, wondering how much pain he had been in and how aware was he? All these things played on my mind, the images of that day remain fresh, it is something I have never forgotten, and I'm sure I never will.

As instructed, I presented myself at the Mortuary at 1000 the next morning. The Mortician was preparing the body. The Pathologist came to do his grisly work. The man was 33 years old, well built and six feet tall. As the Pathologist went through his procedures, I was standing well away smoking furiously to try to overcome the smell. The Pathologist called me over as he dissected the man's lungs. 'He smoked and this is what it's done to him already.' He tipped up the bottom of the lungs and out came a black tar like gunge. 'That tar reduces the lung capacity and irritates the membranes which causes cancer and a large number of other medical problems.' I put my cigarette out! I'd like to tell you that I gave up smoking then and there, I did a few years later and I certainly never forgot what he showed me, and have quoted it to others many times.

The HGV driver was reported for traffic offences, originally causing death by dangerous driving. However, in the absence of evidence of dangerous driving, that was reduced to driving without due care and attention. He pleaded guilty and received a fine and a 6-month driving ban. What price taking a life? The dead man's family were outraged at the leniency of the sentence, and who could blame them?

For most of us it is rare to be on foot on a motorway, it is illegal unless there is an emergency, so we rarely encounter vehicles moving at 70 mph plus. At that speed vehicles come upon you so quickly it is very difficult to judge. Traffic Officers are well used to it and very careful. The same dangers apply to major dual carriageways and it was on one of them that we attended one very foggy morning. Vehicles descended a steep hill into Brightstone and as they reached the bottom, they entered a dense fog bank. Before long, there was a serious accident in the fog, and the same happening all around the town. I found myself at the bottom of this hill, wearing a reflective jacket, trying to slow vehicles as they entered the fog bank before they ran into the accident. The trouble was that the fog seemed to be creeping up the hill and obscuring the warning sign that we had placed, so that I soon found myself standing in fog in the middle of the road! Vehicles came out of the fog and saw me at the last moment and there was much squealing of brakes and a few skids. I tried to stay below the fog bank, but it was very difficult. I had to stay on the balls of my feet to leap out of the way when necessary.

I have to say it was one of the most frightening experiences of my life, and probably madness. The traffic officer I was with was engaged elsewhere, or I'm sure he would have given me some potential life saving advice. As it was, I had no radio and no further signs and if I left the scene, a serious accident was almost inevitable. I don't know how long I was there for but it seemed like an eternity. I don't know if you can picture a large HGV emerging from the murk, seeing me, braking and going into a skid with its trailer snaking round behind it! Thankfully, none of them turned over and the fact that I'm here to tell the tale shows that none of them hit me, but it is most certainly an experience I never want to go through again!

The rest of the traffic attachment passed without anything much of note happening. I did have a good chuckle one day when we were gathered in the Traffic Office. One of the men came in who had been chauffeuring an Assistant Chief Constable around. He told us of an incident when he had upset the ACC and was vigorously chewed out. He then proceeded to tell us what he thought of the ACC in very uncomplimentary terms and concluded by saying; 'that ACC is a right bastard.' He hadn't seen our frantic gesticulating going on as we saw the ACC arrive behind him! 'Thank you for your opinion Mr Edwards, now perhaps you will demonstrate you can drive as well as you can curse.' A very sheepish, red-faced officer followed the ACC out and we all burst out laughing. I wondered what would be said on his staff appraisal! Anyway, the two-week attachment left me very firmly of the mind that traffic was not for me.

That encounter with the ACC reminded me of a story the Chief Constable told. He answered his office phone one day and the conversation went like this. 'Chief Constable.' Lengthy pause, 'you're pulling my leg.' 'No, this is the Chief Constable, who do you want?' 'Stop pissing about, I am through to Traffic aren't I?' 'No, you are through to the Chief Constable, now what do you want?' Lengthy pause as the truth sunk in. 'Do you know who I am?' 'No, I have no idea.' 'Well, let's keep it that way!' Caller rang off.

A few weeks later, I spent two weeks attached to CID, being taken by experienced detectives as they went about their work investigating crime. Some of them were really good at examining scenes, working out what had happened and interviewing suspects and I tried to learn from them. CID officers had an amazing amount of freedom compared with uniformed officers. There were tasks allocated and every morning there would be crime sheets handed out, but after that, they worked as they saw fit. There was a CID diary which they were expected to maintain and leave some indication of what they were doing, but it could be incredibly vague, things like 'enquiries re burglary', what burglary, where, what enquiries? Etc. They rarely took radios with them and in those days, there were no mobile phones. The Detective Sergeants were busy with their own enquiries and the Detective Inspector, well, he kept an eye, when he wasn't having a drink or playing on a fruit machine in a local club! Like any group of men there were good and bad, hard workers and shirkers, natural thief takers and others who seemed entirely unsuited to CID.

Many of them had cultivated one or more informants. Giving of information normally required payment and there was a constant tussle to keep the amount given out as small as possible, while the informant did his best to get the amount increased. It was possible to claim back money so spent, but it was far from rare for the amount paid out to the officer to be less than the officer had given the informant, the money thus having to come from his own pocket. Such sources were carefully protected because they were very vulnerable and at the same time very valuable. Because it was a secret matter, rumours were widespread about how people got their informants. It was commonly believed that one of the Detective Sergeants slept his way to a good selection of informants, often preying on prisoners wives. How true it was is impossible to know. Certainly, he had a string of informants producing as much intelligence as he could possibly handle. Informants were a very useful way of gaining intelligence and I made a mental note to look out for one or two for me. I thoroughly enjoyed those two weeks and decided that I would like to have a go at CID at some stage after I had completed my probationary two years.

Shortly after I had completed my attachment, an opportunity arose for me to practice my detective skills. I went to a call about a theft in a shoe shop. The shop hadn't been open long that morning when the Manager discovered that some £70 was missing from the till. A considerable sum then, more than three week's salary for me. I reasoned that as it was from the till it was likely to be a member of staff, and as none of them had the chance to leave the shop, the money may well be concealed on the premises. I persuaded the manager to close the shop, divided all the staff up so that they were all in two's. There was an odd number of staff so I searched with one girl and no one was left alone. Then we searched all their belongings, but without success. Undaunted I asked the manager to tell the staff, still in their pairs, to search the shop, every nook and cranny, every shoebox etc. After around 20 minutes, the money was found in a top shelf shoebox. Feeling rather pleased with myself I then set about interviewing each member of staff in turn, asking them where they had been, whom they had seen where and so on. Gradually a picture emerged of two women who were the only ones in the vicinity of the till and the hiding place without others around. More questioning and I was pretty sure I had my man, or rather woman. Unfortunately, I couldn't extract a cough, i.e. get a confession. Nevertheless, I was able to go back to the Station and hand the case over to CID with it almost tied up. An experienced DC arrested the woman and she eventually confessed her crime. A feather in my cap and hopefully an aid to a later application to work in CID.

A year passed very quickly with my enthusiasm for the job undiminished. After I had completed 15 months service, it was time for a continuation-training course of four weeks at Fireford Training Centre. This was a brand new establishment, which took over from Burrstone, which was closed down. We were the first students in this new centre. Back to classrooms and lectures, struggling to stay awake, physical and self defence training etc.

We had an interesting session exchanging incidents we had dealt with in our short service. My making an arrest on the first day and facing an armed man soon after, together with being complained about three times, was of considerable interest, that was until an officer from the Airport Police told of his involvement in the crash of a civilian passenger aircraft, which had resulted in considerable loss of life. His description of the state of some of the bodies was absolutely awful, so much so that I am reluctant to pass on the details even now.

In one lecture the Sergeant asked, 'how many of you have sworn at a member of the public?' Not surprisingly, no hands were raised; no one was going to admit that! 'I don't believe you,' continued the Sergeant. 'Clearly it is usually wrong to swear at people, but there are times when it might be appropriate.' He went on to tell us of an occasion when he was out on patrol with a young well-educated Constable. It was night duty and they were in the main street of the town when they saw a drunken man staggering up the middle of the road, cursing and gesticulating at passing cars. The Sergeant told the young Constable to deal with him. The PC approached the man and said, 'excuse me sir, you really can't behave like that, I must ask you to desist and come with me to the pavement.' The man glared at him through bleary eyes and then took a swing at him. The Sergeant had to go to his aid and the man was arrested and carted off for a night in the cells.

A few weeks later, the Sergeant was out with an experienced Constable. They were in the High Street, it was pub turning out time and yes, there was the same drunken man meandering along the middle of the road. The Sergeant told the PC to deal with him. The PC walked purposefully up to the man, who happened to be Irish, drawing his truncheon as he did so. 'Listen Paddy, if you don't want this big stick shoved up your fucking arse, you will go home, and go home now!' 'Yes shirr, yes shirr' was the reply and the Irishman obediently disappeared off home. Our instructor made the point! It is important to speak in a language that the person we are talking to clearly understands. It is also important to be forceful when the occasion demands, to be obviously in charge. Being apologetic is rarely the right course; it can too easily be taken as weakness.

As on our original training course, we had sessions on the use of drugs. Not only the law, but also the opportunity to see, touch and smell some of the drugs being sold and used in our police areas. We could not handle some drugs like LSD because they can be absorbed through the skin, and we were absolutely forbidden to embark on the dangerous practice of tasting drugs as TV Detectives do with great regularity.

To emphasise the danger of drugs we were shown a film. I had been shown the same film on my initial training some 15 months before. It featured eight drug addicts, all now off the hard drugs they had been addicted to, showing how they bought, concealed and used drugs. With a struggle, I managed to stay awake for this second showing, but was brought to full attention when the Instructor told us that the eight people were all now dead. Since the film had been made they had all gone back to drug use and had all died, from drug poisoning, organ failure through drug use and fights between rival drug gangs. What sadness and misery drugs bring, they are the motive for so much crime, they do untold damage to physical and mental health and they undo values and standards of behaviour in people. People who were once respectable, law-abiding citizens are driven to behave in an utterly selfish and destructive manner. I saw too much of it during my years in the police and since.

At another session on the continuation course, we were asked to outline our procedure if we saw a suspect vehicle. Many of us talked about checking that it wasn't stolen and then taking no further action. As the Sergeant pointed out, the owner might not have reported it yet, or it might have false plates and made the point that there was an increasing danger that officers would rely on developing technology rather than the old style skills, which were still necessary. Car thieves were getting more and more cute. There had just been an incident in Brightstone where two thieves were pushing a stolen vehicle to bump start it and were approached by a police patrol. They got the police car crew to help them! If a police officer stopped a suspect car, he would ask things like, 'what is the registration number? Without looking, what is the mileage, what is in the boot, what month does the car tax expire?' Thoughtful villains had got to know this routine and had written the answers on their cuff or used a felt pen to write all these details on the inside of the drivers door, below the officers sight line but just right for the driver to look away from the dials but yet know the answers.

The Sergeant related a story of when he was a young PC being sent out on patrol with an experienced officer. They stopped a suspect vehicle and questioned the driver to see if the car was his. He had the right answer to all the questions but the experienced officer knew something wasn't right. He thanked the man for answering his questions and put him at ease by talking about cars and the weather and the like. Then he said that he'd better let the driver go and stood back before saying, 'oh one thing, will you put the radio on for me?' The man lent forward and put his hand out to turn on the radio, but there wasn't one and he was nicked!

They were good skills, and there was, and probably remains, a danger of them being lost. It was a story that has always stayed with me and made a point worth taking on board for all of us. A good philosophy was, if you see anyone or any vehicle that looks worth a check, check it, and check it thoroughly, however difficult it might be, e.g. going the other way etc. Don't just rely on computer checks.

All training is useful and the course helped me as I had started studying for the Sergeant's examination, which I could take after two years service. There was a test at the end of the course and I managed to do very well and was the top Larkshire student. It all should help to get me safely through my probationary period.

Chapter 7 The End Of Probation

After my four week holiday at the Training Centre it was back to the Station and back to shift work and patrol duties, still most of the time on beat patrol in the town centre. At night there were still the youths, still trying to bait me, but not as much as before our little confrontation and I had learned my lesson and refused to rise to the jibes. One evening a group of them were walking along the other side of the road, calling insults to me across the traffic. They had clearly had a drink or two and were showing off for the girls among them. One of them decided to demonstrate his athletic prowess and attempted to leapfrog a parking meter. I say attempted, because he didn't make it, instead, a very delicate part of his anatomy collided with the top of the meter. He hung there briefly, suspended in mid-air and then fell heavily to the ground. I really enjoyed that and made no attempt to hide my hilarity from the group, as they helped the fallen hero to his feet.

One busy day a Sergeant from our Station was walking back through the town centre from the Crown Court. As he walked through the shopping centre, he encountered a group of youths who insulted and threatened him. He identified the leader of the group and knocked him to the ground with a hard straight punch in the face. Bleeding from the mouth and nose, the youth was helped away by his mates as they beat a hasty retreat. Members of the public were there in numbers. Some were obviously shocked but most of them clearly felt that justice had been done. One would have thought that these lads were beginning to learn, but some of them had still not got the message.

I've mentioned Paul before. He had many years of service under his belt and only very rarely did foot patrol, usually being on mobile patrol either in the town or in the rural area. One evening he came on foot patrol with me in the town centre. We soon encountered the local lads who were after a bit of fun. A group of them walked straight towards us intending to force us off the pavement to make way for them. As they came within range Paul's arm shot out, grabbed the nearest one by the throat, shook him a little and then threw him on the ground and trod on him. 'Oh, did you get in my way son.' Paul said. One of the others said, 'you're only tough because you can hide behind that uniform.' 'You think so do you, well lets go round the back of the shops, I'll take my uniform off and we'll see how tough you are.' They didn't want to know and beat a retreat.

A little later, we came across them making a nuisance of themselves in a shop doorway, falling into passers-by, embarrassing women and their usual range of infantile behaviour. Paul approached them, 'what do you think you're doing?' 'Sheltering from the rain, ain't we,' one of them replied on a fine clear evening. 'Right, that's it' said Paul and set about them, throwing them all out into the street with kicks, punches and vigorous shoves. On the edge of the pavement stood a newspaper seller, muttering to himself, 'I can't see nothing, I can't see nothing!' 'Now clear off and if I see you again you can expect a good hiding.' They all ran away and for the rest of that evening made themselves scarce. If we did come across any of them, Paul threatened and manhandled them, dispersing them and encouraging them to spread the word that the gloves were off, and they could expect tough treatment at every stage. This approach worked, the word did spread, and I never had the same problems with youths again. In fact, talking to colleagues they all found that the problem was greatly reduced. It seems Paul had sorted it out for us in just one evening!

One of the offences I hadn't dealt with was drinking and driving. I nearly had in the unfortunate incident with bumpers, but anyway I took the view that I would act if someone's bad driving drew my attention to them. However, if I stopped them in a routine check, or for some other reason and then detected alcohol on their breath, I wouldn't act unless there was something in their driving or manner that concerned me. The law gave much wider powers than that and some of my colleagues vigorously imposed the law but it wasn't my favourite offence. It was pointed out to me that it was about time I detected an offence which is frequently committed. On the following night duty, I was on foot patrol in the town centre when I saw a car being driven the wrong way down a one-way street. I stopped the car, smelt alcohol on the driver's breath, required a breath test, which was positive, and arrested the man. I called up for a vehicle and we were conveyed to the Station.

Back at the Station, I explained the reason for the arrest to the Sergeant, who was our section Sergeant, the ex-military man I mentioned earlier. The procedure then was to wait some 20 minutes, require another breath test and if that was positive require a blood or urine sample for laboratory analysis. While we waited, there were forms to complete about my prisoners circumstances. It was mentioned that he was ex army and Sergeant Frank asked him about his service. They discovered that they were in the same theatre of war at the same time, and they were off, recounting the good old days and swapping stories of some of their adventures. Time passed and I couldn't get a word in edgeways. Eventually I pointed out that more than 20 minutes had passed and the Sergeant, fairly reluctantly, agreed that a breath test should be required. The motorist provided a breath test, the Sergeant took the tube, examined it and declared that it was a borderline case and in the circumstances, a caution would suffice. With that, he threw the tube away before I had a chance to check it myself! I'm sure it was as the Sergeant said, he surely wouldn't have allowed a shared past to influence his actions, would he?

A couple of nights later I was on mobile patrol with a colleague, when we saw a car being driven at high speed through the town, we followed it signalling it to stop which it didn't. We turned off into a residential estate and the vehicle pulled up outside a block of flats. The driver ignored our calls and ran inside. The door locked and the only way in was at the invitation of a resident. It was 0100 in the morning and we had no idea where the man lived. We checked the car, which was all in order apart from the smell of alcohol. A check revealed the flat number but he wouldn't answer the buzzer. It looked as if he had got away with it; by the time we got to him, he would probably be under the limit or drinking at home. Before we left we decided to teach him a little lesson so we let all his tyres down. That should help him remember his behaviour and we were pretty confident that he wasn't going to complain! Was that poetic justice or just improper behaviour?

Some time later, we were on a council estate when we saw a car being driven by a disqualified driver. He drove off and we chased after him. He refused to stop and drove into an industrial estate, which went down to the river. He abandoned the car at the edge of the estate and ran off down an alley. We searched for him without success. We decided that we ought to immobilise his car, so we let down all his tyres. We returned the next day to find his car jacked up on bricks with all the wheels gone. Someone had obviously thought the car was dumped and helped himself. Well, he should have stopped for us and the state of the car now would make it more difficult for him to drive while disqualified again! To add to his woes we visited him at home and reported him for driving while disqualified and no insurance. He told us about the fate of his car, we were of course surprised to hear it, 'well if you will abandon your car in such a foolish place, what can you expect!'

After the last incident with a driver who had been drinking and who turned out to be an ex-soldier, it was a little ironic that a few days later I arrested a serving soldier for drink driving. I was alone on mobile patrol around 0130 in the morning when I encountered a car stalled in the middle of a junction, the driver got the car going only to stall again. He restarted the engine again and clearly had trouble remaining on the right side of the road. I stopped the car and found the driver to be as drunk as a lord, unable to even speak properly and hardly able to stand up. He was an Army Staff Sergeant on his way to somewhere north of London to visit his girlfriend, after a night in the mess having a very good drink. I arrested him and took him in, to face the same Sergeant. Whatever our Sergeant might have thought we both knew that there was no way this one wouldn't be positive and had to be properly processed. After being dealt with, it was many hours before he was sober enough to be allowed to go home. He duly appeared in court where he was disqualified from driving and given a hefty fine for being some three times over the legal limit.

I hoped that this case would remove that obstacle from my path and I could return to my own standard of enforcement. It was not to be. I had to deal with a drink driving case that led to a complaint, the man who had snatched my truncheon and I had pushed into a dustbin, related in Chapter 4. It was a bad mistake allowing my truncheon to be snatched, and demonstrated again how much there was to be wary of and how much there was to learn, a process that would continue throughout my service. My goal was to get to the position of being reasonably confident that I would be able to cope with any situation. If I didn't know what to do, I hoped, in the words of a TV advert, 'to know a man who does', even if I didn't possess the knowledge myself.

Public perceptions are an area where there was much to learn. On one early shift, the traffic lights failed at a major junction in the High Street and I was sent there to do traffic duty until they were repaired. When I arrived there was a lot of traffic and as I walked into the middle of the road I was welcomed, 'About time, come on, sort this lot out,' 'At last, never find a copper when you need one,' etc. I did my best to sort things out and keep traffic moving as I waited for repairs. As time passed there was no sign of relief or a repair crew, and it gradually dawned on me that something had gone wrong and I had been forgotten. My radio wasn't working so I just continued doing traffic duty and was there for over four hours. I hoped that someone would notice that I was missing but it was not too be.

As I continued with the traffic duty, the traffic flow became heavier and despite my best efforts, the traffic built up. I began to get comments like, 'ah, a Policeman, I wondered what was causing the problems,' and, 'why don't you get those lights repaired, they're a lot better at it than you,' and other such helpful remarks! It was clear that the police were to be blamed if they didn't do traffic duty, and blamed if they did! I was standing there in the middle of the road doing my very best, becoming more and more tired with the arm waving and concentration. My efforts were totally unappreciated by a critical public, and yet if I left, they would complain that I was failing to do my job. After over four hours I'd had enough and left them to it, ignoring the complaints as I left. I went back to the Station and some other poor officer was sent out to take my place.

In reflecting on that lesson, I saw that I must simply do my best irrespective of the views of the public, some would understand and some wouldn't. You really can't please all of the people all of the time!

Inevitably, there were a number of sudden deaths to attend. More often than not, a neighbour would report curtains closed and milk on the doorstep, or mail and newspapers building up. I would try to raise the occupant by shouting, knocking or ringing, peer through any available windows in the hope of finding something and then look for someone with a key or try to contact a relative. If that was not possible, I had to get in, either through an insecurity or by forcing an entry, and then, steeling myself, seek out the occupant. I found some not there; they had gone to hospital or a relative and forgotten to cancel their deliveries. Some I found ill, fallen on the floor and unable to move and was able to get them to hospital. Others I found dead, in bed, on the floor, in an armchair, or in the bathroom.

In one of my first such cases I got into the house only to find that I couldn't get into the bathroom, something was behind the door, I eventually forced it open enough to look round and saw an old chap collapsed on the floor, clearly dead. I managed to move him enough to get in, and saw that his face was contorted with pain and he had nearly bitten right through his tongue. I examined his body for signs of violence but there were none and the house was secure, with no sign of forced entry.

He could have been poisoned in some way so I called out CID as well as the Police Surgeon. No one was quite sure and the Doctor agreed that poisoning was a possibility. The scene was preserved until a post mortem could determine cause of death. That pm revealed that he had been suffering from bowel cancer and had been to the lavatory and strained, his bowels had burst, and the contents had indeed poisoned him. That wasn't the technical terms employed, but that was the substance of it. Poor old chap, we didn't tell the family of his dying agonies and the funeral directors were able to do a good job of making his face look peaceful.

In another case, I found the occupant in the lounge where he had collapsed. He had fallen forwards and his face had fallen onto the electric fire. Fortunately, the house hadn't been set on fire, probably because the electricity had run out in his coin-in-the-slot meter. However, there was a terrible injury to his face with all the skin and tissue burnt away on one side. Even in this case, the family were able to view his body at the Hospital Mortuary. They were kept outside of the room and looked through a window towards their dear departed, who was carefully positioned so that his good side faced them.

As the end of my probationary period neared I could look back on two years during which I had dealt with a variety of crimes, many traffic incidents, sudden deaths, lost children, public order problems, pub fights, car chases, domestic and industrial disputes, an armed offender, people with psychiatric disorders, dangerous dogs and a shot cat. If I related them all, this book would probably be as long as Encyclopaedia Britannica. Perhaps I will just add one or two tales about the incidents just mentioned that haven't figured yet.

Lost children were always a matter of great concern. There have been too many times when police have missed a child hidden nearby, or not been thorough enough in checking suspicious people nearby. Thankfully all the incidents of lost children while I was at Brightstone ended happily.

On one occasion, we had a report of a missing three year old from a council flat on an estate. Officers attended and the usual enquiries and searches were begun, while others stayed with the worried parents.

Then a call came in reporting a small child standing on a high window ledge in a nearby block of flats. I volunteered for the call and sped off. I wasn't the craziest of drivers, preferring to get there safely rather than being dead on time! This was an exception however and I drove at great speed. I scattered a flock of pigeons and hit one in a loud and feathery impact. I carried on along a two lane, one-way street. As I screamed along the road, there was a cyclist on my nearside. He heard my siren and roaring engine, panicked and fell off the bike. He fell outwards into the road right in front of me and I was almost on top of him with my nearside wheels about to run over his head! Somehow, I braked, swerved, and missed him by the smallest margin possible. I screeched to a halt, shaking and terribly shocked. If I was shocked, what about the poor cyclist! After ascertaining that he was ok, I leapt back into the car and raced off, just a little slower. I arrived at the flats, where there was no sign of the little lad. A few minutes later, he was found safe and well and returned to his mother.

I could have killed that cyclist and all for nothing, what a terrible thought, but what a dilemma police sometimes face. If the lad was on the window ledge, and I drove fast enough I might have arrived in time to save his life, and if I'd driven slower and more carefully and he fell?

Fast driving is a necessary part of police life but is very dangerous and needs to be moderated so that speed is combined with safety. In car chases, it was all too easy to lose sight of that prudence. One night duty I saw a Mini Cooper that looked worth a check. As I went after it, the driver took off. My Hillman Imp was no match for the Mini but I did my best, cornering on two wheels, accelerating fiercely in low gear and trying to tell other patrols where I was. I managed to keep the car on the road and the Mini in sight, although with too high a quota of frights. Suddenly a police Rover 3500 overtook me and screamed round a tight bend with the tail of the car in a controlled skid just avoiding colliding with parked cars. It quickly ran down the Mini, the driver tried to run off but we soon caught and arrested him on suspicion of stealing the vehicle. I was wrung out and shaking from the experience and full of admiration for the traffic driver who had demonstrated some great driving.

We had all survived, but it could so easily have been a different story. After a number of cases where there were serious accidents after car chases, we were told to disengage from pursuit if the driving was too dangerous. Easy to say, but very difficult to do. Once that was realised the Duty Inspector in the Force Operations Department was given the responsibility of calling off a chase if he felt that it was too dangerous.

I don't know how many road accidents I attended but it was certainly too many. If it was a damage only accident, it seemed to me that the police were doing the job of the insurance companies. If the drivers were at odds, we apportioned blame and perhaps prosecuted one of those involved for careless driving or the like. If convicted of careless driving, guilt had well and truly been apportioned and there would be little point in further argument. The paperwork for an accident report took several hours and the whole thing was better settled by insurance.

Injury accidents required more investigation and care. Seat belts were not compulsory and no one had heard of crumple zones or ABS brakes. Thus, there were more facial injuries, which often looked much worse than they were due to the amount of blood loss. Most accidents were serious matters, causing injury and/or furious exchanges between those involved. However, there was room for some accidents to be amusing.

A woman driver (no comment about women!) had parked her new car in a line of cars. The car was automatic and she had never driven an automatic car before. When she returned to the vehicle she claims she was boxed in, it was impossible for us to know. She got into her vehicle, put it into reverse and tried to ease slowly backwards. Instead, she reversed back sharply and collided with the vehicle behind. She quickly put it into drive, accelerated too fast and collided with the car in front! In a panic, she put it into reverse, shot back and hit the car behind. This time she hit it so hard that she drove it into the car behind. In a real panic now, she put the car into drive, hurtled forward, hit the car in front and pushed that into the car in front. She had now damaged four cars and was in a real panic. Back into reverse, she crashed into the car behind so hard that it collided with the car behind, which then collided with the car behind. Back into drive and yes, you've guessed it; she collided with the car in front, which collided with the car in front, which collided with the car in front. Having damaged six cars, she decided that was enough! She managed to back up safely, into drive and out of the line of vehicles, the trouble was she still accelerated too fast, sped across the road, straight through a garden fence and ended up in a front garden!

We were called and attended this amazing scene. The driver was very shocked and apologetic, but unhurt. She pointed out that she had only just got the car with automatic transmission and that's why it happened, a simple accident, 'and you're not going to prosecute me are you?' Unfortunately we did!

I actually witnessed the following accident. I was in a line of vehicles driving into town. A few vehicles further ahead was a bus, which pulled into a bus stop. There was sufficient room to pass the bus and vehicles began to do so. In front of me was an Austin Maxi, driven by a woman (I'm really not getting at women). It came to her turn to pass the bus, but she misjudged it and ran into the back of the bus. She reversed back and had another go, got it wrong again and crashed into the back of the bus. Bits fell off the front of her car as she sat there trying to collect herself. The bus driver leant out of his window and looked back at her with an amused smile on his face. She reversed back and tried again, and crashed into the back of the bus again, with more bits falling off of her car. She hadn't got it wrong by an inch or two; about two feet of her car had collided with the bus.

At this point, I got out of my car and told her not to try again but to pull into the kerb. She managed that. The bus only had a scratch on its rubber bumper; the driver didn't want any action taken, so I waved him off. The poor women's car was extensively damaged but just about driveable. She lived just a little way along the road, so I let her off with a warning and watched her carefully drive off down the road. There didn't seem much point in prosecuting her, explaining to her husband and to the insurance company would be fun enough!

Of course, accidents do happen to men. One of my colleagues was driving in the outside lane of a two lane one-way street. There was a single decker bus in the inside lane which wanted to turn right, and needed to swing out wide to do so. The bus turned and the police car was squashed against a lamppost! The driver was uninjured but the car was a sight to see. The bus driver alleged that the police car was travelling too fast, the police driver that the bus driver hadn't looked. The officer went back to the car behind him and spoke to the driver. 'I need witnesses; you must have seen what happened?' 'Yes, I did, it was your fault!' A Sergeant attended and took details. An indignant PC was prosecuted, convicted of driving without due care and attention, fined and his licence endorsed. As if that wasn't bad enough the police took his driving permit away for six months! Bad luck in such circumstances if the witness doesn't like police!

Trouble in pubs was something we had to deal with quite regularly. A landlord had the right to exclude anyone he or she wished. They had the duty not to serve anyone who was drunk. The Licensing laws had some interesting twists. It was an offence for an employer to pay his employees their wages in a pub. It was an offence to play cards for anything but very small stakes. It was also an offence to allow prostitutes to gather. Most of these laws were designed to stop hubby spending all his wages before he went home to the good woman. I attended a few domestic disputes where the husband had done just that and the disgruntled wife had hit him with a frying pan or the like.

Back to the pubs, attending a pub fight was exciting as a young policeman. But often dangerous. On one occasion a colleague and I attended a pub fight, when we went in we were met with a volley of bottles and glasses, which caused us to conduct a prompt withdrawal! With assistance we went back in, the fight was over, some of those involved had gone out the back and no one had seen anything!

When we had to arrest someone or physically remove them we were very vulnerable. There is not much room in most pubs and while we were busy with the man we were trying to arrest, we could be kicked, punched and spat on, and sometimes were. It was usually impossible to know who the culprit was. Another regular problem was the macho culture in many of the tougher pubs. The man we wanted to evict or arrest didn't want to lose face in front of his mates. So where he would probably have come quietly if we had arrested him outside, inside he would fight and struggle. I wasn't the expert at these close quarter struggles; I did my best, but lacked the techniques which made the job easier. Paul was very good at delivering incapacitating punches or kicks, and several others were adept at judo and floored their man quickly and efficiently. Speed and efficiency were important, because some of the other customers would be tempted to join in against us, and a prolonged struggle increased the likelihood that this would happen.

Wild west style major fights with people thrown through windows and chairs being broken over people's heads were very rare. The trouble was usually stopped before it could get that far. We did have a couple of good scraps where bottles and glasses were thrown and we were seriously outnumbered. However being in the town meant that we just had to hold our own for a few minutes and help would arrive. It was an encouraging and bravery enhancing fact that we would nearly always win in the end. During my time at Brightstone, a number of officers were injured at disturbances in public houses, but none of the injuries were serious.

There was a large Mental Hospital in Brightstone. It was not uncommon for their patients to wander off and we would go looking for them. I met some very interesting characters amongst them, their reality was impossible to penetrate, yet was clearly so real to them. I found one old lady wandering down to the town centre. I picked her up and asked her where she was going. She told me that she was going back to Glasgow, where she used to live, and would I take her there. I agreed, turned round and drove back the mile or so to the Hospital. After five minutes or so, she said, 'isn't it taking us a long time to get to Glasgow.' As I pulled up outside the Hospital she asked, 'is this Glasgow?' 'Yes, this is where you live.' 'Well thank you very much for the ride, you have been most kind.' With that, she meekly went inside with a member of staff. Most of them I came across were like that, very few were violent but some could be extremely violent, often unexpectedly. Normally we would return them to the Hospital, even if they had been up to mischief. There was little point in prosecuting them for shoplifting, assault or any other relatively minor misdemeanour.

On a couple of occasions, I returned patients to the Hospital at night. I found it a most disconcerting experience. The hospital was a forbidding grey stone building dating from the Napoleonic Wars. Inside the standard of decoration was poor and the corridors and wards echoed to footsteps and a variety of noises from patients. While I was there, a patient started screaming hysterically, which set off some others. Other patients were clearly frightened and curled into a ball or pulled the bed clothes over their heads. Staff came to restore order and settle them back down, and the noise subsided to a background hum and moan and other indeterminate noises. On another occasion, one patient was continually wailing loudly and thrashing about at some imaginary foe.

I had to return a patient one afternoon and as I talked to staff at the door of the ward, a woman came running towards us shrieking wildly. Staff intercepted her and dragged her away. 'What was the matter with her?' I asked. 'Oh, she has a thing for men, especially men in uniform, if we hadn't stopped her, she would have leapt on you and tried to rip your clothes off!' Really! I thought I had better have a look at this woman, after all whatever was wrong with her, she had good taste! As they were calming her down I managed to have a look at her, she was about 50, with a moustache and very hairy legs. Not quite my type.

So there I was with two years of experience under my belt. I felt I had acquired a good level of experience, my supervisors agreed and my appointment was duly confirmed. I had made it, a fully-fledged copper at last! I still very much enjoyed the work and felt that this was the career for me. I would take the promotion exams as soon as I could and the future looked bright.

During my two years probation I had a proud record of never being late for duty, it was close occasionally but never once late. Within days of completing my two years of probation my wife gave birth to our first child. I was present at the birth and left the hospital that night absolutely delighted. I got chatting to another proud dad as we left the hospital and we decided to go for a celebratory drink. It turned out that this guy was a professional villain, on bail at that time, and with several prison sentences under his belt. When I found out that he was a villain and he found out that I was a Policeman we had a good laugh. Not the usual reaction I can tell you, but we were both on a high.

After a good chat and a few beers, we left the pub to walk home. He lived near some friends of mine and as we walked by, we could hear that they had a few friends in. On impulse we dropped in, I introduced my new friend, omitting his past, and drinks were pressed on us amid all the congratulations. Well one thing led to another and it was gone 0200 before I set off to walk home, slightly the worse for wear! I had to get up at 0430 for early turn, nowadays there is probably paternity leave, but not then. Anyway, I set two loud alarms and quickly fell asleep.

The next thing I knew was that it was 1000 hours and I had slept through the alarms and should have been at work more than four hours ago! I had no phone at that time, so I got dressed, walked to the nearest phone box and rang in to say that I was unwell. Asked why I hadn't rung in before I explained that I hadn't been well enough to make the journey to the phone until now. Hoping that had done the trick and feeling rather guilty, and rather hung over, I returned home.

Within a very short space of time, there was a knock on the door and I opened it to see an Inspector and Sergeant. They wanted to know what was going on, I didn't quite understand what the fuss was about and explained again. Then they told me that when I didn't turn up at 0545 officers were sent to the flat but were unable to get a reply. Other officers came around 0800 and tried again without success. They had managed to rouse all the other occupants of the block of flats on both occasions, but not me! As a consequence, the Inspector and Sergeant suspected I wasn't at home and wanted to know where I was. I could only stick to my story and say that after a bad night I must have been so sound asleep that I didn't hear. That at least was true! Saying they were far from happy about it, they departed. I didn't particularly know the Inspector and Sergeant, if they had been the ones from my section, I would have told them of the circumstances confidently expecting them to understand and be forgiving, but I couldn't take the chance with these two. There were no further repercussions apart from a black mark on my record, but they were rather special circumstances and I hadn't been late had I? Well not really!

Chapter 8 Animals

As my career progressed, I was constantly confronted with new experiences and frequently reminded of the gaps in my knowledge and experience. Of course, as with life itself, that would be the case no matter how long I served. New things were one of the joys of the job, and at the same time one of the trials. I attended a call one day where two large Alsatians had torn apart and killed a small dog belonging to a very distressed old lady. I tried to remember what my powers were. The owner of the dogs wasn't present but lived nearby. I knew I could report the owner of the Alsatians for failing to control them, but could I confiscate the animals, in order to prevent a recurrence? I could not remember but I was reluctant to admit my lack of knowledge over the radio and reasoned that there must be such a power in the relevant Act.

An RSPCA Inspector was on the scene with his van, so we put the dogs in the back and off we went back to the Station. I explained my actions to the Station Sergeant, who looked horrified. 'You can't do that; you have no powers to bring them in unless you can't locate the owner. Could you locate the owner?' 'Well, yes, but.. .' 'No buts, you will have to take them back.' Somewhat red faced with embarrassment we put the dogs back in the van and returned them to the owner. I have to admit that I pretended that we had taken pity on him and were returning his dogs on the condition that he kept them under proper control.

I wouldn't want anyone to think that police work consists of whizzing from one incident to another. Sometimes it can seem like that, but at other times, nothing much seems to be happening. It is then important to develop good self-discipline in order to keep alert and working, rather than subsiding into apathy and boredom. I was very rarely bored, but it was sometimes pretty routine. I usually enjoyed going out on patrol, but going out on foot patrol on a freezing morning at 0600 wasn't a joy, nor was foot patrol in the early hours of the morning with cold rain slanting down. On a really cold night or early shift it was just impossible to stay warm, my body clock was telling me I should be tucked up in bed under a warm duvet, not wandering round the deserted streets in case some villain was as crazy as me. More than once I stood in a shop doorway thinking, 'there must be a better way to earn a living'. The thought didn't last and if I was on mobile patrol, the car roof provided a metal umbrella and there was a heater, so things were much easier. Some men wore women's tight on cold nights under their trousers, but I was too concerned that I might be hurt and have to reveal all to hospital staff! Over the years police officers had developed a number of ways of keeping occupied in the quiet times, especially in the wee small hours, supervisory officers did not approve of most of these activities!

One of my colleagues had a catapult and was wont to go to the local park where he took pot shots at birds and squirrels! Others had found themselves warm dry places to shelter, and probably fall asleep, some would use the time to study while out parked up somewhere. We were wont to play pranks on each other. A favourite was to discover a colleague's patrol vehicle while the occupant was away and to turn on the blue light and siren switches. When the officer returned and turned the key in the ignition a terrible noise resulted which made him extremely unpopular with the residents nearby! When there was snow or frost about, it was great fun to skid the cars around on the frozen grass in the park, trying to outdo each other for the length of a skid or the number of spins. I have to admit that on one occasion I hadn't closed the passenger door properly. As I spun round it came open, dug into a bank and was badly bent! How was I going to explain this to the Sergeant? We took the car to a colleague's house, got his tools out and bent the door back into shape, trying not to make too much noise. In the dark it looked reasonable, just a little crease! Thankfully, I got away with it.

Occasionally a dog handler would use a quiet time for training which involved us. I'm not particularly fond of dogs, especially great big ferocious Alsatians. I quickly learned that they could not recognise police uniforms. If there was a chase and a dog was sent into action, it would run down and attack the nearest running person, as an officer was usually behind offenders chasing them, the officer was in grave danger of becoming the target. One had to hope that you heard the dog being released; the handler would always shout a warning, whereupon it was a very good idea to freeze and pray that the dog would run by. If an offender was brought down by a dog there was a strong likelihood that he would need stitches, usually in an arm but a leg or even a posterior would do just as well!

A couple of times when I was on foot patrol in the middle of the night, one of the dog handlers would call me on the radio to ask me to help him train his dog. I tried to say no, but I got little choice. He would send the dog to find me, and I would desperately try to find somewhere where the dog couldn't reach me. Towns are not good places for dogs to follow a scent trail but they are better in the middle of the night because there are fewer smells around. If I could reach the back of shops a fire escape ladder was a safe haven, if I couldn't the nearest bolt hole would do, like a telephone box. The dog always found me and when in a telephone box the glass seemed very thin as the dog snarled and barked at me outside.

This 'fun' was usually carried out around 0300, and when it was over, we would retire to the Police Station for a regular 0400 cup of tea. The handler, Fred, would get his dog out in the yard, and call out, 'who's first for tea? I am, get 'em boy.' Whereupon this savage animal would run at us seeking a target and we would scramble back into our cars and remain there trying not to show fear. Fred would get his tea and then nonchalantly come to the door and call the dog in, and we, very cautiously, went in for our tea.

One of the other dog handlers Gerry, was a real character. He got in serious trouble after one incident. He joined other officers in the pursuit of a stolen car. Eventually the car crashed and the two occupants made off. Gerry sent his dog after them and the dog quickly brought the first man down. Gerry took him back to his van and put him in the back. That part is agreed, what follows is not. According to the arrested man Gerry asked him who his mate was, he refused to say. Gerry asked him a couple more times without success. Then he got his dog and said, 'if you won't tell me, tell my dog.' With that, he put the dog in the back of the van with the man. The dog did what dogs do, bit him, several times. In several places. The offender very quickly volunteered the name of his colleague, who was duly arrested

The injured man was taken to hospital for treatment of his wounds, which necessitated several stitches. He was then released back into police custody. When he had been dealt with, he made an official complaint about Gerry. An investigation was set in motion. This resulted in Gerry being arrested and he was eventually charged with causing grievous bodily harm with intent, a very serious offence. The case ended up at Crown Court and lasted five days. At the conclusion, the Jury went out to consider their verdict. It took them five hours before they returned with a not guilty verdict. A great relief all round, especially for Gerry who had been facing the loss of his job and a prison sentence. He had denied the offence of course, saying that the injuries had been caused when making the arrest. That must be right, he couldn't possibly have done what the car thief had alleged, could he?

Dangerous dogs, stolen cats, straying sheep or cattle, injured animals etc were frequently brought to our attention and required attendance and careful handling. Their fate can arouse strong feelings as I found out one day when I was on duty in the Station office. A man came in holding a cardboard box containing an injured squirrel. The RSPCA was closed he said, so I agreed that he could leave it with me. The squirrel had a broken back and clearly couldn't be helped and the kindest thing to do would be to end its suffering. The duty Sergeant came with me as we took the squirrel out into the yard. There the Sergeant got a spade; I laid the squirrel on the ground face down and stretched its neck out. One blow with the sharp end of the spade severed the spinal cord and brought instant death. We took no pleasure in it, but felt that we had taken the kindest course. We disposed of the body in the dustbin and I returned to the Station office to find a drawing above my desk with a picture of me being hanged on a scaffold, underneath was written, 'Squirrel murderer'. Obviously, someone didn't agree with our course of action, and I found that I had been sent to Coventry and I didn't even do it!

I was sent to investigate a report of a child bitten by a dog. The dog had been running free in a park and had bitten a little girl on the ankle, and she needed medical treatment. The indignant parents had made enquiries and knew where the dog lived. I went to the house and was invited in. I asked the owner if he had a black and white mongrel, he confirmed that he did, so I told him of the allegation. He protested in the strongest possible terms that he had owned the dog for years, it had the most wonderful nature, was the best pet he had ever had, and in all the years it had been with him it had never even snarled at anyone, yet alone bitten them! 'I'll prove it,' he said and opened the kitchen door with a flourish. Out came a black and white mongrel, which promptly ran up to me and bit me. I knew I didn't like dogs. I eased it away from me with a gentle foot movement! The owner was duly reported and would have a chance to explain to the magistrates.

In the early hours of one morning, I was patrolling on an industrial estate when I left the car and walked quietly round the back of the buildings pausing to listen every so often. I passed a factory surrounded by a six-foot wall and gate and thought I heard something. I climbed up the wall and looked over. At first, I couldn't see anything but then I caught sight of a movement by the factory wall and a small red light. I climbed carefully over the wall and made my way cautiously towards the movement. As I neared, I heard a low growl, which rapidly got louder and turned into aggressive barking, clearly from a large dog. With a sinking feeling I realised the movement was a guard dog and the red light was its eyes. It came for me and I turned and ran. I didn't know I could run so fast and I've never jumped a six-foot wall before, but I did on that occasion. I leaned against the wall to recover as the dog kept up its furious barking. Whew, that was too close for comfort! Do I like dogs?

I returned to the factory in daylight and saw that it was a large long haired Alsatian, which didn't look at all friendly. I could see then that it was chained to the factory wall and couldn't quite reach the perimeter wall, and I thought I had escaped because of my speed of thought and movement!

A black dog was very much part of police life. Too many times a police vehicle was damaged and the driver informed his Sergeant that the accident had been caused by a black dog. The dog suddenly ran out in front of him and in trying to avoid it, he swerved into a lamppost, or hit a brick wall, or collided with a stationary car. Sometimes they hit the black dog, sustaining substantial damage. Despite the injuries it must have sustained the dog was able to run off and couldn't be found. Amazingly, this black dog appeared all over the force area, and in all its accidents it was never found! Eventually a message was sent round the force from the Chief Constable announcing that the black dog was now officially dead. Therefore, the dog would not be involved in any further accidents and could not be used as an excuse!

I've mentioned a colleague who took a catapult with him on nights to fire at squirrels and birds. Another colleague was not very fond of cats. One night duty he was on foot patrol in the town centre when he saw a cat strolling up the street. He drew his truncheon and threw it at the cat. The cat was too quick and was gone; unfortunately, the truncheon bounced on the pavement and went straight through the plate glass window of a clothes shop, setting off the alarm. The offending officer was last seen desperately trying to reach his truncheon before a Sergeant or hard hearted colleague arrived! Serve him right for mistreating a poor cat. Cats had a bad name amongst some of us because they were responsible for striking fear into the heart of officers on a fairly regular basis. Walking quietly round the back of shops or factories a blur of fur would suddenly flash past in the darkness and it always took a few seconds to calm down and realise what had happened.

I was driving very near the town centre one night duty when a fox suddenly ran out in front of me; I had no time to avoid hitting it. I stopped the car and went back to where the fox lay, still alive. I drew my truncheon intending to try to put it out of its misery, when it gave a last convulsion and died. What was I going to do with a dead fox, I wondered? As I looked round, I saw a row of terraced houses; some of them still had dustbins outside from the collection earlier that day. I picked up the fox by its brush, crept over to the nearest house, gently lifted the dustbin lid, dropped the fox into the dustbin, and replaced the lid before leaving the scene, chuckling as I went at the thought of the householders face in the morning!

Some years later, I was sitting in a headquarters canteen relating this story when a civilian woman employee from the other side of the room shouted out, 'so it was you! I live there and found a fox in my dustbin one morning and wondered what on earth had happened.' I had to humbly apologise, to the amusement of the assembled company as I remembered the old maxim, 'be sure your sin will find you out'.

If a rapid response was needed in the rural area, especially at night, there was an increased danger of colliding with animals. Serious accidents were likely if the driver couldn't keep his nerve and strike the animal rather than swerving or braking too fiercely. Every instinct calls out to swerve, but safety dictates otherwise. I only remember this happening to me once. I was travelling along a straight stretch of country road reaching 80 mph when I caught a rabbit in my headlights, sitting in the middle of the road, I could only grip the wheel tightly and with a sickening thud strike the rabbit and continue to the call. I was very sorry about it and thankful that it happened only once. Other colleagues had struck bigger animals such as a fox or a badger. It was amazing what damage the collision could do to a police vehicle.

Against that was the joy of watching animals at night. Seeing a badger searching amongst the trees or a family of foxes playing in the moonlight. I was once lucky enough to catch an owl in my headlights as it swooped down and caught a mouse for its dinner. On another occasion, I rounded a bend at dawn, just as a kestrel crashed into a hedge after a small bird. For something rather different, I several times saw a bull servicing a herd of cows as dawn broke over the fields. What stamina! I'm told that the farmer has to remove the bull or it will continue until it drops dead from exhaustion

From time to time, we came across injured animals, usually as the result of road accidents. We would always call the RSPCA if we could, but often they were so far away, if we called out a Vet, who would pay? Nevertheless with an animal in obvious distress urgent action had to be taken. I soon discovered that foxes and cats have such strong heads that a truncheon is likely to do no more than stun, not kill them. The spade carried in emergency vehicles was an effective dispatcher. When it was necessary to kill an animal I made a point of not telling the civilian women in the Station, who were doubtless responsible for my identification as a squirrel murderer. I hated doing it but sometimes it was necessary to be cruel to be kind.

Of course, the encounters we had were not always with small animals, from time to time we had to deal with horses, cattle or sheep that had escaped onto the road. Thankfully, I never had to deal with an animal of that size that had been seriously injured. We did keep a captive bolt gun at the Police Station to put down large animals. However if at all possible, the RSPCA or a local vet was called out.

If you are a horsey person dealing with horses is fairly simple. If not then you have a problem! Straying horses are not easy to round up and being called to deal with three of them in an industrial complex proved beyond my skills. I sought assistance and one of my colleagues arrived. He caught hold of one horse by its mane, leapt up on its back and rode it bareback to the field it had escaped from. The other two meekly followed, and I was most impressed!

I was looking forward to my bed at the end of a night duty when I was directed to cattle on one of the main roads leading into the town; I duly attended and found a herd of cows strolling about all over the road. I tried to shepherd the cows back down a side road towards their field, no joy with hand waving etc. I had a brain wave; at least I thought it was. I got back into my Hillman Imp and used it to gently push the cows, revving the engine loudly to intimidate them, it seemed to be working and I got them off the main road and down towards their field. I even managed not to get any dents in the police car. I got to the field and just as I was congratulating myself, they saw a narrow footpath, which ran alongside the field and all followed each other on to the path and broke into a trot. Expletive deleted!

I drove round to the next point where the path emerged onto a road. I left the car and walked down the path towards the advancing cows. They didn't seem to be paying much attention to me, still trotting towards me. I took my helmet off and waved it and started shouting, still they came forward. I blew my whistle, waved my helmet vigorously and ran towards them. They just continued trotting towards me. The path wasn't wide enough for me and the cows to pass each other, so it was a game of chicken, whose nerve would break first? Yes, you're right it was me! I jumped and clambered up a prickly hedge and just got out of their way in time.

As they trotted on and out into the road again I considered my options. It was now well gone 0600 and I should have been tucked up in bed. The early shift should now be on duty so I radioed for help and two more officers joined me. Back to guiding the cattle with our cars, out onto the main road and back down the correct side road, this time blocking the entrance to the footpath. We got them back into the field and gratefully closed the gate which some idiot had opened causing me all this trouble. Then it was back to the Station to go off duty, apologising to the guy who was waiting for my car, a) for keeping him waiting and b) for the rather unpleasant brown smelly stuff, which was smeared on the front of the car.

I can't leave the subject of animals without relating a story that I was told, I had no personal experience of this one but it deserves retelling. Patrolling officers came across an Irishman who, with the aid of a wooden box to stand on, was engaging in an act of bestiality with one of two ponies in a field. He was found to be very drunk, was duly arrested and the following day appeared before the local Magistrates. Discussion arose about which of the two ponies was the subject of the man's attention. The Chairman of the Bench asked the Irishman if he could clear up the question and he replied, 'yes shirr, it was the brown one.' 'How can you be so sure?' 'Well shirr it was the best looking one!'

Chapter 9 Responsibility

Now with a little over two and one half years service under my belt, I was trusted to be a tutor Constable to new recruits. It was either an honour, or a sad reflection on the willingness of some of my senior colleagues, or even our supervisors opinion of some of them, I wasn't quite sure which. Anyway, I was happy enough to do it and try to pass on some tips from my vast experience! My first charge was Mike, 19 years old and as keen as mustard. I took him up to the Mortuary to witness a post mortem on his first morning and collected him a few hours later. He was a little green but seemed to have coped well enough with the experience. He wanted to know if we had many dealings with death and I told him how uncertain police work is, it is impossible to know what is coming next, but dealing with death will be part of it.

I think he was still in his first week when we were directed to an address where the elderly occupant had not been seen for a few days. Enquiries revealed that he never went anywhere, the curtains were closed and milk left on the doorstep. None of

JAMES CANNON

the neighbours had a key and no one knew where his family lived. I forced a window at the back, got in and let Mike in the front door. We found the occupant lying dead in the bathroom wearing only a pyjama top; the trousers were lying on the floor. It appeared that he had got up in the night to use the toilet, stood up, had a heart attack, which led him to collapse full length on the floor where he died. Our job was firstly to check for any signs of violence, and then act for the coroner until the coroner's officer takes over. The old chap was in the throes of rigor mortis so was not very easy to move, but with my help, Mike examined him and found no sign of violence.

I decided that we should carry him into the bedroom and lay him on the bed and put his pyjama's back on. I took his feet and Mike his shoulders and we lifted him, ready to manoeuvre through the bathroom door. Unfortunately, because he was rigid as a board when I lifted him, I must have gone slightly forward and he pushed back on Mike who toppled backwards and fell into the bath. I couldn't hold the old chap just by his feet so he fell into the bath on top of Mike! As he fell, he went onto his side and then toppled right over so that he was face to face with poor Mike. I shouldn't have laughed but I couldn't help it, it was quite a sight. I recovered my equilibrium and together we moved the body enough for Mike to clamber out. I'm not sure who had the whitest face, Mike or the old boy, but his face was a picture. I told him we always try to arrange something like this for new recruits so that they can get used to dealing with death!

Mike recovered very well and had a good story to tell. He worked hard and learned quickly, making it relatively easy for me to help him through his first six weeks before he could patrol alone. He went on to build a good career and it was nice to think that I had helped in some small way.

My next probationer was Karl. He was much quieter and less confident than Mike, and I had to work much harder to help him do things. There are so many circumstances where the people we deal with will pick up on someone who is unsure and hesitant and seek to exploit it. Karl found that in his dealing with some of the troublesome youngsters and in other situations.

We were on mobile patrol one day and pulled up in the middle lane at a set of traffic lights as the lights changed to red. A car flashed by us in the outside lane and drove straight through the red light, which by now had been red for perhaps three seconds. It was too dangerous for us to follow immediately but we went after it when the lights changed and caught up with the car five or six miles further on. Karl had the job of interviewing and reporting the driver. The driver turned out to be a very confident solicitor who completely denied going through a red light. Karl was very hesitant but with a little prompting reported him correctly.

When the case came to court, the solicitor pleaded not guilty and defended himself. In accordance with usual practice, we were called in to give evidence one at a time. Karl was very nervous and I did my best to put him at ease. He went in first and was in the witness box for some 45 minutes, I learned later that, as I expected, most of that time was taken up with cross-examination. He came out of the court looking rather shell shocked. I told him to come back in with me and sit at the back while I gave my evidence.

I was then called and went in and gave my evidence. The defendant solicitor then stood up to cross-examine me. 'I put it to you that you were looking for offences for your young companion to deal with; when you saw me go through an amber signal you decided that will do.' 'I saw you drive through a red light.' 'I understand you are tutoring your young colleague?' 'Yes, sir.' 'Isn't part of your remit the task of finding offenders and either reporting them or if appropriate making an arrest?' 'Yes, sir.' 'It must be difficult sometimes, and the pressure must build as time goes by without the required results?' 'I'm not aware of that, sir, and anyway there are always enough offences being committed for us to deal with.' 'Oh, come on officer, there must be lean times, when you need some luck?' 'Luck obviously plays a part, but it is the luck of being in the right place, at the right time to observe an offence, rather than forcing our own luck by fabricating evidence.'

After a lengthy pause, he changed tack. 'What was the make of car next to you in the nearside lane?' 'I don't know'. 'What was the car behind it?' 'I don't know.' 'What was the car behind you?' 'I don't remember.' 'Well, what was the first car coming the other way when the lights changed?' 'I don't know.' 'It seems to me that you don't know very much at all do you?' 'All I do know is that I had stopped because the lights were at red, and I saw you overtake me and drive through them while they were clearly showing red, and there is absolutely no doubt about that in my mind.' That clinched it, he was duly found guilty, fined, and his licence endorsed. I talked it through with Karl, told him the story of Sergeant Frank's evidence, went through what he had said and tried to encourage him in that he had obviously stood up under questioning, so that we got the right result. I hoped that such experiences would build his confidence.

One of the things most Policemen dream of is actually catching an offender in the act of committing a crime such as burglary. One night we responded to a call about intruders on the premises of a house on the edge of a pleasant out of town estate. We were quite close and rushed to the scene. The woman of the house was at the door, screaming and agitated, so we rushed in to be confronted by two men fighting. One of them was completely naked so I guessed he must be the householder! They were in the lounge, crashing into furniture; quite a bit of it was now overturned and probably damaged. I joined in the fight, pulled the offender off, forced him down and managed to hold on to him. Within a minute or so, other officers arrived and the burglar was overpowered and handcuffed. We refrained from making any comment to the man of the house about his pyjams! He and his wife were both shocked but uninjured. They had heard a noise in the middle of the night and the man came down to investigate surprising the burglar. I think I might have put a dressing gown on first!

I would have liked to have given the arrest to Karl but he had dithered at the back. While I was talking to him, the offender was placed in someone else's car and one of the other officers claimed the spoils. It was my arrest really, but being a humble chap, I didn't make a fuss about it. That incident of catching an offender red handed was the first and only time that it happened to me as a PC. So much is luck, just being in the right place at the right time. Talking to criminals over the years confirmed how much is simply a matter of good fortune, and also how often police have prevented an offence, simply by walking past the site of an intended crime. We never knew about it and such events never appeared in any statistics, but were a valuable part of police service.

Unfortunately, Karl didn't improve much and eventually left the service before his probationary period ended. I was very sorry that I hadn't been able to help him more, and felt that a 50% success rate was not very good. Fortunately, I didn't lose the confidence of my senior officers and continued with the training.

Every new police officer looks forward to some of the excitement they have read about, seen on TV or imagined. There is a real adrenaline rush when driving fast to an incident with sirens sounding and blue lights flashing, in a chase on foot or in a car, in a pub fight or incident of public disorder, in discovering a crime and making an arrest etc. For some of us, especially keen young recruits, these incidents are rarer than we might have wanted but hope springs eternal. I probably didn't help with my charges when I told them of some of the exciting incidents my colleagues and I had been involved in. I tried hard to find them the exciting incidents they craved and there was a lot of rushing around, there were a few chases, and rushing to scenes with lights and sirens blazing, but more often than not, the incident turned out to be less than reported.

A man seen breaking into a house turned out to be a householder trying to get in after being locked out. A terrible fight turned out to be horseplay between friends, a person about to jump from a high building turned out to be the window cleaner, a body floating in the river turned out to be a log etc. Each time our adrenaline was fired up and expectations were high only to be dashed. Understanding the stress these non-events engendered was really possible only for colleagues who had been through similar experiences. Many of us sought each other's company for a pint to relax after shift work, especially the always-busy 1400-2200 shift. For new recruits this was another opportunity to listen to stories from their experienced colleagues of what they might expect and perhaps have their expectations raised still further.

There were of course times when something dramatic and exciting did happen, and the next two probationers I had were able to be involved in incidents that were a little out of the ordinary and provided some excitement that they could look back on. They could also join in the story telling with the next generation of recruits.

My next charge was a young Scotsman called Dan. He was a very likeable lad, keen to learn, perhaps not the brightest star in the firmament academically, but a good man who showed reasonable common sense and was promising. We had a steady flow of incidents to deal with, some we were directed to and some we found ourselves, but nothing of too much note, at least for a while.

We were on mobile patrol on a busy night duty when we were directed to trouble in the local park. We arrived to find a group of Hells Angels fighting with a number of local lads. We were heavily outnumbered and could expect little backup as everyone was busy on other calls. Dan went to rush into the middle of the fight but I held him back, 'let them see us, hopefully when they do the fighting will stop and then we can disperse them.'

Our presence was soon noticed and the fighting did subside. Then we walked between the opposing groups and told them to disperse. As we were right in the middle of them, one of the Hell's Angels lashed out at a local youth and they started fighting. I pulled them apart and forcefully told them to stop and go home. The local lad obediently turned away. The Hell's Angel turned to face me and without any warning kicked me in the groin. As any man will know that causes extreme incapacitating pain, but I knew that to go down in the middle of this lot was to invite a good kicking. Dan drew his truncheon but I told him to put it away, it wouldn't do much good against such overwhelming odds and would only inflame the situation. Bending forward slightly in some pain from the kick, I told the man I was arresting him for assaulting me. He reacted by punching me in the face, roaring like a wild animal and charging me. I stood back and brought my heavy three cell torch crashing down on his head with all the force I could muster, so much so that the inside of it burst out. It had no effect and he kicked and punched as I fought to restrain him. Other men joined in the attack and Dan did his best to hold them back. As I struggled with this very violent man in the middle of this melee, I was struck hard on the back of the head, again and again, so that I could feel my blood running down my neck. They say you see stars in such situations and my vision certainly was impaired, it would have been so easy to go down under the blows, but some instinct of self-preservation kept me on my feet.

Dan had managed to call for assistance, making it a priority call. When a priority assistance call went out, everyone dropped what they were doing and went to their colleague's aid. I didn't know that Dan had made the call of course, all I knew was that I was fighting, if not for my life, then certainly to avoid serious injury. I was dizzy with the blows to my head, pain in my groin and to my face and legs from the punches and kicks. Eventually the cavalry arrived, the group was dispersed and officers helped me subdue my attacker, and two or three of the others who had been helping.

Apart from the principal attacker, we had to let the others go with a severe warning as I couldn't tell who had been hitting me. We had sufficient grounds to have arrested them all, but there were too many of them, and prudence dictated we leave it. A girl stepped forward and admitted hitting me on the back of the head; she had used a crash helmet, held by one of the straps and swung over her head. She was the sister of my attacker; both were arrested and taken back to the Station. At the Station it was obvious that I had a number of injuries, fortunately Dan, although very shaken, was unhurt.

One or two of my colleagues, enraged at the incident were all for giving the man a good thrashing in the cells. I forbade it, telling them that I wanted them to appear in court uninjured while my injuries would be obvious for all to see. I hasten to add that beatings in the cells were not a regular feature of police life. I was then taken to hospital for treatment. Most of my injuries were cuts and bruises, but I needed a number of stitches in the wounds to my head, and my left arm had been badly wrenched and needed treatment and rest. I went back to the Station to write my statement and then retired from duty. I went home looking for sympathy and instead got told off for bleeding on the pillow. Such is life!

The next morning I went down to Brightstone Magistrates Court for the case against my attackers. I gave my evidence and then Dan made a good job of giving his. The Bench retired to consider their verdict and returned after a short while to find them guilty of assault occasioning actual bodily harm, and resisting arrest. The Chairman of the Bench then proceeded to sentence. He began by saying that this was the worse case of violence against police that he had ever come across in his 18 years on the bench. Very promising I thought, should be a lengthy custodial sentence coming up here. To my enormous disappointment, he went on to sentence them to 200 hours community service each. What a let down, and just to rub it in, they disappeared from the town and never did any of the community service. So much for relying on the Bench for justice!

After a couple of day's sick leave, I returned to duty healing up nicely. Whether I could ever father children again I didn't know! However, Dan had a good story to tell and had seen some action. My arm has never been the same since. I had to fill in a form registering my injuries for the Department of Health. As a result, I had to appear before a medical board where it was adjudged that I had a permanent 5% disability to my arm for which I was awarded a one off payment of £35 and 2 shillings, which was about £35.10p in the new fangled decimal currency. What would I spend such a vast sum on? Thankfully Dan wasn't put off by the incident and continued to do well in our time together. We became firm friends and he made a good copper and served his full 30 years.

The last probationer I worked with in this sequence was Peter. Young and keen, well educated and bright, he had all the early indications of a lad who could go far. We found a good amount of work for him but nothing of any particular note until we received a call one evening around 2100. The manager of a pub on the outskirts of the town reported that he was having trouble with a man, who he believed was armed with a knife. We sped over there and went into the bar. Other people had been cleared out of the area to avoid the man except for a woman next to him. They were both sitting on stools at the bar, and he was holding a long bladed knife. I approached him carefully. As with a mad dog it is vital to show no fear, whatever you are feeling inside, and a positive way to do that is to stand close enough for him to strike with the knife if he so chose, trusting that my reactions would be fast enough to get out of the way if he did strike.

I looked into his eyes and saw that he was either very drunk or under the influence of drugs. I asked him what the problem was and he answered, 'I'm going to kill you, copper,' as he did so he waved the knife in a threatening manner. I managed not to flinch and replied, 'that's nice, why would you want to do that? What is the problem?' He muttered something about the world being all fucked up and the police were part of the problem. I tried again to ask him why he had a knife and what did he want, with no better result. I talked to him, asking his name, where he lived and so on, but got little sense from him. I was looking for a way to distract him, as it was fairly obvious that I wasn't going to talk him into putting the knife down. I asked him what he was drinking, he told me the brand of beer, and then I suggested he try the beer behind him. Thankfully, he turned to look at the pump and I took the chance to jump on him, grab his wrist and try to wrest the knife from him. We had a short, vigorous struggle, before I got the knife and told him he was under arrest.

As I did so, from the corner of my eye I saw a sudden movement from the girl. I turned to her, still sitting next to him, she reached down into her sock and produced another knife and she lunged at me with it. I could see that she too was high on drink or drugs. I managed to avoid her lunge, shouted to Peter to look after the man, grabbed her arm, bent it back and wrested the knife from her, before telling her she too was under arrest. With the help of Peter, we forced them both face down on the floor, handcuffed them and wrestled them out into the car park and into our car. They continued to struggle, the man boasted of being an expert in martial arts and threatened murder, disembowelling and other dire consequences for my actions. He kept that up all the way to the Station, where others helped us deal with them and put them in a cell to allow the effects of whatever they had taken to wear off.

I found I was shaking like a leaf and needed to sit down. Peter complimented me on the way I had dealt with them and said, 'I was right behind you all the time'! I asked him if he was frightened and he said that he was frightened for me. 'That's very nice Peter, thank you.' 'Yes if they'd stabbed you I was next!' Actually, he had done just the right thing, standing by to help if necessary and not provoking an attack and I told him so. He was very pleased that it had gone so well and looked forward to sharing his tale with others.

The following day we were called up to the Chief Inspector's office. 'I want to congratulate you two on the way you handled that incident in the pub last night, you are both a credit to the police service and I am recommending you for a Chief Constable's commendation for bravery.' 'Thank you, sir, we were only doing our job' (one has to be modest!). 'Don't be so modest, I saw it all.' 'Saw it all, where were you then sir?' 'I was having a drink in the other bar and watched you deal with it.' I tried not to blurt out, 'then why the hell didn't you come and help us?' As if guessing what was going through my mind he continued, 'yes, you were doing so well that I decided not to come and interfere!' I was speechless and after a little conversation with us both and encouragement for Peter, we departed.

Sure enough, we were given a commendation. The details of our 'bravery' were posted on Force Orders and we had to don our best uniforms and parade before the Deputy Chief Constable. We had a nice little chat with him and received our embossed certificates of commendation. I have kept mine to this day.

Incidents like that do happen from time to time, and of course, it's very rare for a Chief Inspector to be watching. In consequence, commendations are pretty infrequent, and in many ways are a matter of luck that someone in a position of authority is aware enough to instigate the procedure.

Peter continued to do well in his six weeks and I really expected him to build a fine career. He took me home one day after work on his powerful motor cycle, and frightened the life out of me. Sadly, just a few days later he had an accident on his motorcycle, his injuries didn't appear too bad at first, but he had severe internal injuries and died before he got to hospital. I have never been on the back of a motorcycle since. His funeral is an enduring memory. His fiancée and family trying to be brave, police pall bearers and a guard of honour of uniformed police. The Deputy Chief Constable, who had talked to us about the commendation just a few weeks ago, sat among the mourners, and an Assistant Chief Constable, who knew little about him, gave a very good and professional oration. A tragic waste of a young life.

Chapter 10 CID

S hortly after finishing my two years probation, I put in an application for CID. To determine suitability it was usual for an officer who showed some potential to be appointed Temporary Detective Constable and serve with CID for a six-month evaluation period. I was fortunate to be given such an attachment after less than three years service. I expect it was more a matter of a lack of applications than the promise I showed. At the same time, another officer, Tim, began his CID attachment and we worked together for most of the six months. I had fondly imagined that we would spend some time with experienced detectives to learn the ropes. Instead, we were told to get out of the Station, to go round the town, find information, get to know local villains and make some arrests.

Our task was rather easier said than done. We followed likely shoplifters, but we always picked a day when they were behaving. We lurked in car parks where a lot of cars had been stolen, all we found were courting couples, whose ardour was somewhat dampened by our intrusion, especially when we checked the girls age! A car was stolen from the car park we were watching, but we missed it. Unfortunately there was a lorry fire at the same time and we were dealing with that. We kept a sharp eye on local youths, who we found to be on their best behaviour. We scrounged bits of information off others and tried really hard.

There were a series of burglaries in a nearby village, now swallowed up by suburbia. The offences were all committed during daylight hours and were very bold. On two occasions, the thieves had been trying to move heavy articles they had stolen. To help them they had put the articles on an armchair and wheeled the armchair to the end of the drive, loaded their vehicle and left the armchair in the road. We had to wonder about community spirit, none of the neighbours ever saw anything. We spent many hours wandering round the lanes of this village. Again, we were out of luck although the crimes did stop, so maybe the thieves saw us around and were put off.

We spent every lunchtime and most evenings in rough old pubs, pubs frequented by local villains who we tried to get to know. The problem arose that it's just not on to drink half-pints, or orange juice, because we would have stuck out like sore thumbs. Instead, we had to drink pints of beer. We would have three or four at lunchtime and three or four in the evening, six to eight pints every day. What a hard life! We had to pay for it as a rule, although on rare occasions we could claim expenses if we were on authorised observations or cultivating an informant.

Despite having to put up with all this hardship, after our first six weeks, we had nothing to show for it, not one single arrest made, and we were becoming rather downhearted. Suddenly the tide turned. A good number of the locals knew who we were despite our plain clothes and consumption of pints, as one old lag told me, 'we can smell a copper a mile off.' We walked into a pub in the middle of the town, as we did a man saw us and ran out of the far door. Completely shedding any pretence at anonymity, we ran after him, knocking people and beer out of the way. Our beer consumption had not slowed us down much and we caught him and took him back to the Station. There we found that there was a warrant for his arrest, as he had been wanted for some time for a number of thefts and burglaries, a good arrest at last!

A couple of days later we were driving into the town, listening to the radio broadcasting the details of a stolen car. Just a few seconds later, we saw the car going past us. I couldn't quite manage a handbrake turn but did my best and we sped after the car. It was quite early in the morning and there wasn't too much traffic. The stolen car was much more powerful than the CID car and was pulling away from us. We lost sight of him as he rounded a bend, but when we negotiated the bend, we saw the stolen car stopped by temporary traffic lights. Before the offenders could turn round, another vehicle pulled up behind them, blocking them in. We stopped and leapt out as two men decamped from the car and ran off. Being young and fit, we caught them! Without the temporary lights we would have lost them, our luck had turned!

Over the next six weeks, we had a good number of arrests for a variety of offences ranging from shoplifting to burglary. Most of them were accomplished without too many problems but there were a couple which proved very difficult. We heard a call over the radio about a theft from a shop in the town centre. A member of staff had tried to detain the offender and had been verbally and physically abused as the female thief made good her escape. A good description followed and Tim and I looked at each other, we knew who that was - a certain foul-mouthed anti-police woman that we had come across before.

Off we went to her address, were let in by her daughter and found her peeling potatoes in the living room. She was small in stature but with a very large build. A bowl of water was between her feet to receive the potatoes, her legs were wide apart revealing part of her belly hanging down over her urine stained knickers - lovely. A volley of abuse greeted us as she denied ever being anywhere near the shop in question. We were satisfied that she was the offender and arrested her. She was not going to come quietly, she shouted and swore, struggled, scratched and bit. Nevertheless, we dragged her out to our car as she screeched, 'Witnesses, police fucking brutality, witnesses.' A few neighbours came out to watch and jeer as we handcuffed her, got her into the police car and took her back to the Station while she swore and threatened us with hardly a pause for breath.

We took her into the charge room where she continued her shouting and swearing. The commotion drew a few officers including a Detective Sergeant. He asked us what it was all about and then said he would calm her down. He went in, talked to her, and did indeed quieten her down. She was under a suspended sentence, so conviction for a further offence would result in at least a few months in prison; she was desperate not to go inside and therefore willing to do a deal.

The DS was investigating a series of crimes believed to have been committed by an acquaintance of hers. He got her to agree to inform on her friend and in return he would arrange to have her let off for the shop theft. She gave some good information and the offender was later arrested, charged and convicted. We then had our charge sheet torn up and had to take the gloating woman home. We wondered what she would say to her neighbours, but she covered up by saying that she didn't do it, and the old bill found that out at the nick and had to let her go. As a consequence, the shop never got their goods back or the offender prosecuted, and fortunately never knew what had transpired. The procedure was not exactly according to the rules but I guess it made sense. From then on, she became a police informant, but only for that DS, we were still abused and sworn at. It was tempting to drop her in it by telling the neighbours she was a grass, but personal feelings have to be subjugated to the greater good!

We picked up on a call to a theft in a house and volunteered to attend. When we got there, we met the householder and his wife. They told us that while they were out an intruder had been in and stolen the money from their coin operated electricity meter, but had touched nothing else. Immediately suspicious we went round the house and found no obvious sign of a break in. They were adamant that the house had been secure when they left, so it had to be a burglary. I asked them if they had any children and they told me of their 19-year-old son. I asked if he had been around, but they said he had been at work. I gently wondered out loud if he could have done it? Highly indignant they emphasised their son's honesty. Just then, the son returned home. We asked him what he knew about the theft and he denied any involvement. There clearly hadn't been a break in and I was pretty sure it was the son, so after a few more fruitless questions I decided to arrest him on suspicion of the theft and take him to the Station. The parents were shocked and angry and I think Tim was rather surprised!

Back at the Station, I questioned him at some length but he stuck to his story. Tim wisely distanced himself and I was in grave danger of having egg on my face, I had no real evidence and needed a confession. Fortunately, there was no compensation culture at that time. In the end, I put him in the cells to think about things, in the hope that incarceration would do the trick. Then I went to the CID office and asked an experienced detective to help me. An hour or so later he came with me and we interviewed the youth together. After another tiring session, he finally cracked and admitted that it was indeed him who had broken into the meter and stole the money. Thank heavens for that. He was duly charged and bailed to go home and explain to his parents. Saved by the bell!

Encouraged by that experience I chanced my arm again. There had been a street robbery, a mugging, and the woman who had been robbed gave us an excellent description of the offender. Two days later, I went into a Hairdresser in the middle of town for a haircut. There were three men working in the shop and one of them fitted the description of the offender perfectly. I had time to consider my options as my hair was cut. The attack had happened at lunchtime in a fairly quiet street just off the town centre. I was able to get into conversation with them and found that they took turns having a lunch break. I made out there had been an accident in the particular street and asked if anyone had seen it. They asked what time it had occurred and then worked out who had been on his break at that time. Thus, I found out that my suspect was out and about at the relevant time.

I took him into the back room for a little chat, decided that he was very shifty and uncomfortable with my questions and arrested him on suspicion of robbery. I took him back to the Station, processed him and interviewed him at length. He was adamant that it wasn't him and he hadn't been in the area at the time. I put him in the cells to think about it. Some hours later I interviewed him again, he remained adamant that it wasn't him. The woman had lost her handbag, containing purse, chequebook and credit cards, makeup bag etc, so I decided to search the man's house and car.

Tim came with me as I took him to his house and searched it thoroughly. No luck, and the same result with his car. Back to the Station, more interviewing with the same outcome. I was running out of options, I didn't have enough evidence to charge him, and the time I could keep him in custody was limited. Making an identification seemed to be the best way forward, It was now late in the evening and it was best left to tomorrow so we locked him up for the night and went home.

In the morning, I discussed my options with a DS. We decided to carry out a street identification. That involves having him walk down a busy street where the woman would be, in the hope that she would identify him. Before we did that, I interviewed him again, the DS joined me, and the Detective Inspector even joined in. He would not change his story. I rang the woman and arranged to meet her that afternoon.

At the appropriate time, the woman stood in a doorway in the middle of the street, Tim and I stood at either end, and we got him to walk from Tim to me. Another officer stood with the woman, in the hope that she could point him out, from among all the others in a busy street. Of course, it was vital that we gave her no indication of which one we wanted her to indicate. The suspect walked down the street and to my dismay, it looked as if she did not pick him out. Tim took him back to the Station while I talked to the woman. 'I know the man you meant. He does look very much like him, but he's not the man.' 'Are you sure?' 'Absolutely sure, he is not the man.' Oh dear!

I had to go back to the Station with my tail between my legs, release the man and apologise humbly for my mistake. He was so relieved to be let out that he was quite generous and forgiving. I offered him a lift home but he was happy to walk, so I apologised again and saw him off the premises. Nowadays he would probably have sued the police, but I never heard anymore about it. I did change my hairdresser; I wouldn't want to let him loose on my hair!

I found that there were often occasions when we had little or no evidence. We had either to give up or take a chance, arrest, and interview, knowing it was a confession or nothing. After that experience, I was a lot more wary. Some of my colleagues had developed some imaginative and somewhat dubious practices in order to exact confessions. I only once saw violence used to get a cough and that was only a slap round the face, (which proved very effective). If a prisoner asked for a solicitor, I have seen another officer pretend to be a solicitor and complete with briefcase, interview his client in the cells! The 'solicitors' pitch was that he needed to know the truth in order to best present a cogent defence. Very unethical and probably illegal, but the information provided usually led to evidence that convicted a guilty man. How wrong is that?

One prisoner we had in custody was informed that there was a warrant out for him, and when we had finished with him, he would be transferred to a particular London nick. He became very fearful at the thought, and was willing to do anything to avoid being sent to this London Station. Intrigued we eventually managed to get him to say why. According to him, he had been arrested for some offence and taken to this Station where he resisted all attempts to extract a confession from him. In the end, he was told he would be tried. He was taken into another room where a 'Sergeant Judge' presided over proceedings. Uniformed officers carried out prosecution and defence. He was duly found guilty and sentenced to death! He was then taken out into the exercise yard where he was forced to watch an officer loading a firearm. He was blindfolded and made to kneel, asked if he had any last requests and then felt the cold muzzle of the firearm placed against the back of his head. The firearm was then discharged but the hammer fell on an empty chamber! Totally freaked out, the man was ready to answer any questions and admit anything they liked. I had no way of knowing if this story had any truth in it, but he was genuinely frightened of going to this Station. I'm sure that if it did happen it was an isolated incident, and I certainly never saw anything like that in our police area!

On occasions when there were two or more suspects there was another methodology I occasionally saw used. The suspects would be placed in the cells but not next to each other, there would be an empty cell in between them. Then an officer, suitably disguised and dressed as a member of the public, would pretend to be a drunk and other officers would drag him into the cell between them and leave him there to sleep it off. The suspects thought the drunk was no problem and talked about their crimes across him, while he made notes. That's not illegal; whether it's unethical, I leave for others to decide. There were other tactics like pretending that we had more evidence than we actually had, or playing off one man against another, letting them believe that their accomplice had admitted the crime and blamed them. A well-known tactic, seen often on TV, is the hard man/soft man routine. One officer aggressive and threatening, while the other is kind and considerate.

Then there was the device of arresting a suspect and letting him think we suspected him of some relatively minor offence. Then the arresting officer would leave the charge room and talk quietly to a colleague, but not quietly enough that the suspect couldn't hear. The colleague would ask the arresting officer what his suspect was in for, and when told exclaim that the crime was a rubbish job and then go on to describe the crime they really suspected the man had committed. They would praise that crime as a 'class job' that they couldn't help but admire. On several occasions the offender's voice would ring out, 'I did that!' Wonderful, what would we have done if so many offenders were anywhere near as smart as they thought they were!

One burglar committed quite a number of burglaries. He wore gloves and was very careful not to leave any evidence. Nevertheless, officers went round to his address and arrested him. He was confident, believing that we could not have any evidence. We did though, we had his fingerprints. On his last job, he had put sticky tape across a window and then cut the glass and removed it in one piece. He wore gloves when committing the crime but he had forgotten to wear them when he cut the tape, and had very kindly taped his fingerprints to the glass that he had left at the scene!

One day a DS took me with him to another Police Station a long way from us where we met a woman who turned out to be the wife of a suspect. The DS tried to persuade her to inform on her husband, but not surprisingly, she refused. He then shocked her as he told her a few details of the man with whom she was having an affair. If she didn't give information against her husband, the DS would have to tell him of her affair! That did the trick and we got the information we needed for another successful arrest and conviction.

This DS used to sail a little close to the wind. There had been a series of good class burglaries in our area. CID officers were pretty certain who the offender was but he was very careful to leave no evidence. He had been hauled in, interviewed and both he and his house searched hoping for a mistake, but to no avail. On another search, this DS 'found' a silver spoon from a recent burglary in the boot of the suspect's car. No one could say that he didn't, but for such a careful man as this burglar, it didn't seem likely and the burglar certainly didn't believe he had left it there. Eventually this DS was arrested and sent to prison for three years for corruption over other cases.

In all my time in the police, I saw very little evidence of any corruption, despite some public perceptions. Even the techniques I've just described were very much the exception to the rule. Most crimes were dealt with properly and solved by hard work and dedication rather than tricks of any kind.

I do recall one instance of a colleague's perjury in order to secure a harsher penalty. As a uniformed PC he had gone to a report of youths causing a nuisance. On arrival at the Railway Station, he found a group of youths annoying people. He chased them off and thought that was the end of the matter. However, one of the youths didn't go, he remained at the scene giving the officer a lot of cheek. The PC lost his rag rather and arrested the youth. When he was back at the Station, he calmed down and as he wrote his statement realised that there was not very much evidence against the youth. He was likely to get little more than a slap on the wrist from the Court. He therefore spiced up his evidence something like this. He described how the youth was being rude, abusive and threatening to people. 'You are annoying people and likely to cause a breach of the peace, so stop it and clear off now.' 'Who's going to make me?' 'Look, be sensible, go away now or you will be in trouble.' 'What trouble? I ain't causing any problems.' 'You are upsetting members of the public; you are being rude and abusive, threatening people and frightening women. If you don't stop and clear off I will arrest you, and you will find yourself appearing before the Magistrates.' 'That bunch of wankers, they're a waste of space, old farts who don't know their arse from their elbow!' At this point, an arrest was made.

The Officer gave his evidence in the Magistrates Court, pausing to apologise to the Bench before reporting what the defendant had said about them. Those of us there couldn't help chuckling at their outraged dignity. Surprise, surprise the youth received a much harsher penalty. The arresting officer later admitted to us what he had done. I confess most of us still thought it rather amusing and no one reported him. Such events were thankfully very rare.

It was a widely held view among officers that the law makes life very difficult for the police. As soon as someone is arrested they have to be told that they don't have to say anything, their silence cannot be held against them, they are entitled to legal representation, can only be held for a limited time without charge and many of the techniques I have outlined would make the evidence gained inadmissible. The one thing that doesn't seem to matter is whether they are guilty or not!

Stop and search powers have been curtailed, I believe suspects now have to be given a written indication of why they are being checked, etc. These developments have got worse over the years so that police are more and more constrained by rules, which inhibit arrest and investigation. In the end, I guess society gets the police they deserve. If it is more important to provide endless safeguards for suspects than powers for police, investigations are hamstrung and many more guilty go free than innocent are convicted.

Tim and my duties of searching out offenders for ourselves came to an abrupt end with a major enquiry. A man had been found dead at an out of town factory and foul play was suspected. It was a large factory with several hundred employees. The dead man was found round the back of a pile of pallets with fatal head injuries. The Detective Superintendent in charge wanted every employee questioned, a formidable task. We worked at least 12 hours a day questioning everyone, we found out about a few thefts and scams but nothing to help us with the death. The post mortem didn't help much.

The man had been found on Monday morning, he probably died on Friday afternoon or evening. The head injuries could have been caused by a pallet falling on him, although there was no evidence on any pallets. However, it had rained heavily over the weekend and it was quite possible that the evidence had been washed away. A disturbing factor was that the dead man had been paid on Friday, in cash, and there was no sign of the money or his wage packet.

Having discovered no evidence from our questioning, it was decided that we should do it all again. We went through the entire staff again, uncovered one or two other crimes, but no more evidence of what had happened to the dead man. A great deal of other enquiries were also carried out, but they all drew a blank. The Detective Superintendent decided that it must have been an accident. Other employees told us that some of them hid their wage packets for later collection, so that they didn't drop out of their pockets while they worked. The dead man had put or hid his wage packet somewhere, and that had probably been misappropriated. At an inquest, the Coroner agreed and a verdict of accidental death was duly recorded. Some of us weren't quite so sure but who were we to question the wisdom of our superiors!

At the conclusion of this major enquiry we went back to the CID office and from then on were given crime sheets to investigate, obviously we didn't get any major crime enquiries, but we knew that, and were happy to work on the ones given us. There was still time for our own enquiries as well. Tim and I continued to work together most of the time, but sometimes went with other officers on various enquires. Tim was taken with another officer to the scene of a domestic murder. The husband had hit his wife 27 times in the face with a 5lb hammer! She had suffered terrible and very fatal injuries. When they cleaned her up at the Mortuary in preparation for a post mortem, they found that one of her eyes was missing. Tim was despatched to the scene to see if he could find it! There was a lot of blood and bits of bone and tissue on the floor, but he found the eye under a sofa, wrapped it in his handkerchief and took it to the hospital. A Policeman's lot is not a happy one!

I went with a Detective Sergeant to a bank in a rural village where a robbery had taken place. A single offender had held up the bank, tied up the manager and made off with several thousands of pounds. We did house to house enquiries, interviewed the witnesses and got officers working on drawing up a list of possible suspects while others prepared a photo fit for wide circulation. The DS I was with was to interview the manager and take a statement from him. We took him back to the Police Station where we talked to him at length and the DS took a seven-page statement. I saw nothing wrong and nothing to cause me any concern about the manager's story.

When he had gone the DS said to me, 'there's something wrong here,' I asked him what had led him to that thought. 'Nothing concrete, but I just feel something is not right, let's do some digging.' He then looked into the manager's life and record. At first, there was no sign of anything but then he discovered that many years ago, when the manager was a teenager, he had been in trouble for a theft. This had occurred in a town in the Thames Valley Force. The DS made enquiries about this case and found that the manager had an accomplice when he committed this old offence. He then traced the accomplice and found out that he had a car of the same make and colour as the offender's getaway car.

This man was clearly a good suspect and he was arrested and brought back to Brightstone. He denied any involvement and we had only circumstantial evidence. The DS then tried a new tactic. He hadn't mentioned the sum involved before so he trebled the amount that had actually been stolen and asked the man again if he was involved in the theft of this inflated figure. Our suspect was clearly surprised and when the DS persisted he suddenly said, 'the bastard, he told me the take was only ****!' This man and the manager had cooked up the scheme between them and the manager had hidden the money for later sharing so that even if the accomplice had been stopped, he wouldn't have had the money in his possession.

The manager was arrested, eventually confessed his crime, the money was recovered and they were both convicted at Court and sent to prison. All because of the 'coppers nose' of that DS. I wished I had been blessed with that gift. This DS was a very effective detective and was always making good arrests, helped by an extensive network of informants. In fact he sometimes had so much information that he couldn't deal with it all himself and on at least one occasion he passed the information on to Tim and me.

He told us who was responsible for a recent burglary and who he would approach to fence the stolen goods. We watched the suspect and within a few hours, he left his home and drove over to Downchester with us following him. He waited in a car park and another car drew up, a man got out and they talked together. We waited until some property was being transferred from one boot to another and then sprang into action. We arrested both men and took them back to Brightstone. The property they had been passing between them was stolen, and they were both charged and later convicted and sent to prison.

On other occasions, arrests could be just a matter of luck. I was returning to the Station from an enquiry when I heard uniformed officers directed to a house where someone had been attacked. I wasn't far away and I went as well. We found a 77 year old man beaten within an inch of his life, lying in a pool of blood at the foot of the stairs, he had been attacked and beaten with, among other things, his own walking stick, and his house had been ransacked. An ambulance was summoned and the old chap was taken to hospital. Scenes of Crime Officers and senior detectives also attended to make a painstaking search of the scene. Nothing turned up from the forensic search and enquiries nearby failed to help in identifying an offender beyond a vague description.

After a few days without any progress, I went out with another detective and we decided that we would ask everyone we met if the vague description meant anything to them. After a fruitless couple of hours, we got talking to a prison officer. Sticking to our decision, we shared the description with him, just in hope really. The prison officer said that he knew a man in the prison who fitted the description. We pointed out that this wasn't a lot of good because if he was in prison he couldn't be out robbing an old man. The officer explained that it was possible, because this chap was on the hostel scheme, going out to work every day and returning to the prison at night.

With growing excitement, we went with the officer back to the prison and searched the inmate's room. Hidden in there we found items from the old man's house. We didn't know where the prisoner was working, we could have found out, but decided that the fewer people who knew the better and it should be just a matter of waiting. Sure enough, the prisoner returned at the end of the day to find us waiting for him. We arrested him and took him to the Police Station. Confronted with the evidence he admitted that he had befriended the old chap to get into his house and then robbed him.

His case eventually ended up at the Central Criminal Court in London where he was sentenced to seven years imprisonment. Thankfully, the old chap recovered, at least physically, although I feared the mental scars would last much longer, and I don't suppose he would ever be as trusting again.

Every arrest brought with it paperwork, witness statements, record of interrogation, antecedent history of the defendant, summary of the case and so on. CID had an office staffed by civilians and the case papers had to pass through the office manager. She was a fairly formidable woman who always seemed to find something wrong with my court papers. In my defence, guidance was somewhat lacking. For example, I had to prepare papers for a High Court Judge, so I asked one of the DS's for help. 'Have a go yourself, and one of us will look it over afterwards.' 'But it has to be with the Judge in chambers tomorrow,' I protested. 'Well, you'd better get on with it then,' came the reply!

Sometimes it was necessary to deliver summons or other court papers. There were two uniformed officers whose job was service of summons, warrants and the like, but if the court case was imminent, we would do it ourselves. We had used a doctor in a particular case and needed to serve him with a witness summons.

Tim and I drove out to his fine house in a nearby village. The door was opened by his wife who invited us in and told us that her husband was out. As we were explaining the purpose of our visit, she asked if we would like a drink? 'That would be very nice, thank you.' 'Tea or coffee, or would you like something stronger?' Well, it would have been churlish to refuse so we agreed that we could manage a glass of malt whisky. A tray was duly produced with cut glass whisky glasses and a decanter. We both enjoyed the whisky and said so. 'Are you interested in whisky?' Well, it seemed rude to say no so we answered in the affirmative. 'Would you like to see my husband's cellar?' Of course we would, and down we went to find that the cellar was given over entirely to malt whisky. The lady of the house prevailed on us to sample some of the whisky, and we were forced to try quite a few to get a true sense of perspective, and spent a very pleasant couple of hours there, sampling the Doctor's very fine whiskies. What a nice lady we agreed as we walked, in a fairly straight line, back to our car!

We had begun our CID attachment by spending a lot of time in pubs and that didn't change. In those days, there was no bar in the Police Station but being out and about in the pubs was a good idea, not just for the beer you understand! There was a culture of heavy drinking among quite a few of the officers and several pubs were willing to stay open late for us, and we were able to go to places like a local hotel and drink until the early hours. In addition, there were several local breweries. They were all keen to see us and the security officers had been allocated quantities of beer just for thirsty Policemen. Occasionally these drinking sessions got out of hand. Once we were in a posh hotel when someone's drink was picked up and thrown up the skirt of a skimpily clad waitress. The man who had lost his drink retaliated with a jug of water over the offenders head and then a food fight broke out. A nearby buffet was employed and at the end of it there were vol-au-vents stuck on the ceiling and walls, together with bits of egg, cheese, ham and the like and the floor was littered with bits of food. The perpetrators had to go back the next day and apologise profusely, and fortunately for all those involved there were no comebacks!

Tim and I managed to stay reasonably sober on most occasions. One evening we were out on the town and met some local businessmen we had befriended. A drink together turned into a session and too much alcohol was consumed especially by Tim. He joined one of the men in drinking pints of beer with a double scotch chaser! When the evening broke up I took Tim home, he just about got into his house and I left him to it. I learned later that he had collapsed just inside the front door. His indignant wife had left him there. A little later, he had woken and been ill all over the hall carpet! Realising he would be in deep trouble he decided to quickly clear it up. In his drink-befuddled brain, he got out the vacuum cleaner to perform the task. His wife was not amused! Fortunately, I didn't make a mistake like that, I'm not sure I would have lived to tell the tale.

One of the roughest pubs in the town had an Indian Restaurant next door. At pub chucking out time many of the pub customers moved on to the restaurant and there was often trouble and racial abuse. One evening Tim and I were enjoying a curry in there when we could see that trouble was about to break out on a nearby table. Tim got up, introduced himself and told them to behave or get out. As he was talking to them another man approached him from behind clearly about to mount an attack. I managed to head him off and between us we kicked them out. The manager was absolutely delighted, and asked us if we, and any of our colleagues, would like to come in every Friday and Saturday night and he would provide us with whatever we wanted to eat and drink in exchange for our presence. That seemed a pretty fair deal to us!

A few weeks later, we were in the restaurant and ordered a meal. Just as it was served, seven men on a nearby table ran out without paying their bill. We reluctantly left our meals and gave chase. With the help of other officers, we caught and arrested them all. They were travellers, several of whom had hundreds of pounds in cash on them. By the time we had processed them it was nearly 0200 and two hungry officers bemoaned their lost dinner. Just then, the manager came to the Station with a nice hot curry packaged up for us. What a gent! The happy relationship continued during all our attachment.

As time went by, we became increasingly confident. We had made a good number of arrests, we had developed our interrogation techniques and were quite good at playing the 'hard man, soft man' routine, even our paperwork had improved so that it didn't always come winging back from the office manager. I have to admit that our beer capacity had also improved! We knew that there was a long way to go but we were on the way and I was enjoying it and thinking very seriously of applying for a permanent appointment to CID.

It is a good thing to become more efficient and confident but great care must be taken to ensure that confidence doesn't lead to overconfidence. One day we were given the task of returning a villain to prison. He had been released on licence but his behaviour had not been up to the standard expected and the Home Office had issued a revocation of licence order, which we had to now put into effect. We knew the man involved and had a good idea where he was. If you remember our encounter with a certain foul-mouthed woman who had been stealing from a shop, arrested by us and then released without charge for giving information, well, we believed he was lodging with her. We decided it would be best to visit the address well after the pubs close to give them all a chance to settle down. We wondered about assistance and handcuffs, but decided, in our confidence, that we didn't need either, we would talk him out without too much trouble. As you have probably guessed, things didn't quite work out as we had hoped!

Around half past midnight the next morning, we drove up to the address and knocked on the door. It took quite a while to raise anyone and then the dear lady of the house came to the door. It would be an understatement to say that she wasn't pleased to see us and we were treated to a volley of abuse. We told her that we had come for her house guest who we will call Riley. Despite her assertions that he wasn't there, we could see him lying asleep on the sofa. We pushed past her and went into the room. We woke him, showed him the revocation order and told him we were arresting him, all the while putting up with insults and abuse from the dear lady of the house. Riley looked at us and said, 'wild horses couldn't drag me out of here, yet alone you two bastards.' With that he turned away from us and went back to sleep! The noise the woman was making was obviously disturbing the house and we decided that prompt action was needed. We tried talking to him again but he completely ignored us so we were forced to come up with an alternative plan very quickly.

I told him that if he wouldn't come voluntarily we were going to carry him out, but he simply ignored us. I took hold of his head and shoulders and Tim got his feet, we lifted him up and made towards the door. After a couple of steps, Riley turned his head and sunk his teeth into my thigh. He bit down hard and very painfully and would not let go. I dropped him, but he refused to let go and bit down still harder. I punched him in the head in an effort to persuade him to let go. That did the trick but hitting him was too much for the lady of the house. Still shouting and swearing, she came up behind me as I knelt on the floor, she grabbed the ends of my tie, pulled them either side of my neck and set about strangling me with it. I tried to throw her off, but she hung on grimly. Summoning every ounce of strength I had I managed to throw her across the room. The trouble was that she didn't let go of my tie. Being a very heavy woman I was pulled off my feet, or rather my knees, she landed on the sofa and I landed on top of her!

This all happened too quickly for Tim to do very much and just at that moment the door burst open and the rest of the family flew in. They had a dog which immediately attacked me, Tim struggled with Riley, and the woman's husband and daughters joined in the attack on me, incensed, not only that we had invaded their house in the early hours, but because I had the temerity to make sexual advances to their mum, evidenced by my laying on their mum on the sofa, even if I was on my back!

I managed to turn round and forced the woman's hands off my tie, trying to ignore the dog biting my ankles and the husband and daughters pummelling my back and head, and I managed to stagger to my feet. I was just in time for one of the daughters to swing a pram carriage at me, which hit me on the side of the head. There is a time to advance and a time to retreat and we knew when we were beaten, Tim and I retired in disorder, pursued by the dog and another volley of abuse and shouts of triumph!

Licking our wounds, Tim and I considered our options. I needed treatment so we decided to leave Riley for now and Tim drove me to the hospital. I had superficial cuts and bruises to my head and upper body, dog bites to my ankles and deep human bite marks in my thigh. The nurse was fine when I took my shirt off for treatment to my upper body wounds, but for some reason she found it very amusing when I had to drop my trousers for the bite to be examined and treated! She went out and I heard her say in a low voice, 'there's a copper here with his trousers round his ankles.' A few more nurses came to look and discreetly chuckle, what a cheek, if you'll pardon the pun! Then they left and the original nurse, still suppressing laughter, treated the wound and gave me a tetanus injection in the bum. Struggling to regain some vestige of dignity, I pulled my trousers up, lifted my head high, thanked the staff and joined Tim to return to the Station.

On the way we returned to considering our options, we very much wanted to arrest Riley, would he still be at the house? Was it worth trying again? The good thing was now that it was after 0200 there were no other CID officers around to have a laugh at our expense. We decided we had nothing to lose by a further attempt to arrest him, but thought it might be prudent to go better prepared this time. We went to see the uniform Sergeant and asked for some men. Taking handcuffs with us, three uniformed officers accompanied Tim and I as we returned to the address. With two officers we knocked on the front door, while one of the PC's went round the back. After a lot of banging and some delay, my favourite lady came to the door and greeted us with venom and more abuse. She wasn't going to let us in but we pushed past her and searched the house. The commotion awoke the rest of the family and they came downstairs but made no effort to attack us, being outnumbered this time. They even stopped the dog from biting me, although it clearly wanted to! We found Riley hiding in the bath, under a pile of towels. We arrested and handcuffed him and took him in, the gentle criticism of the lady of the house echoing in our ears!

Riley was placed in the cells and we later charged him with resisting arrest and assault causing actual bodily harm. He was taken to court and had his sentence extended by another three months. He was then taken back to prison to serve his sentence. I was left with a scar high on my right thigh, which will be a permanent reminder of the dangers of over-confidence! For the rest of my police service I never again wore a conventional tie. I got hold of clip on ties and used them, much safer, and the knots looked better than my efforts anyway!

As the end of our six-month attachment drew near it was time to consider the future. I remained keen on CID if they would have me, Tim was less sure. I discussed the matter with my wife where I ran into a slight problem. During the six months, I had done a lot of overtime, at least 20 hours a week and often more. We weren't paid directly for overtime but an aggregate was worked out over the month for all CID officers. If that aggregate reached 8 hours a week, but less than 12 hours, a small payment was made.

If we managed to average 12 hours or more, a larger payment would be made. The average was always above 8 hours, and often exceeded 12 hours. On top of the overtime, we had done a fair bit of socialising. In consequence, we might leave home at 0730 and not return until the early hours of the next day.

We had a young child, just one year old and my wife was pregnant again. She needed help and resented the time I had spent away from home. I tried to persuade her that it wouldn't always be like this, but I didn't do very well! After much discussion, she said that it was either CID or her, I couldn't have both! I didn't have a lot of choice really, so I never did put in an application to join CID.

It's idle speculation to wonder whether they would have accepted my application for a permanent appointment. Admission is through a selection board with the result far from certain. I don't think the Detective Inspector was over fond of me, I hadn't bought him enough beer over the club! Perhaps unfair, but I did not have a high opinion of him. On one occasion, he had come into the detention room and interfered with an interview I was carrying out with a suspect, and he only made things worse. He had made no effort to find out what was going on before blundering in. Other than that, he said nothing to me at the beginning of my attachment, he rarely spoke to me at all and I hardly saw him for the whole attachment other than in the club drinking and playing on the machines.

Although there seemed no prospect of a career in CID, I really felt that the six months on CID were certainly not wasted; I had thoroughly enjoyed the time and learned a lot.

Chapter 11 Back to uniform

Following the end of my six-month attachment to CID It was back to uniformed shift work. I must admit that I felt unsettled by my time in CID and wondered what else I might have a go at. The Inspector realised that I was a little unsettled and we had a chat about it. He asked what would be my favourite option for duty. I told him that I would love to crew the emergency car. On each shift there were a number of panda cars, usually single crewed, with radio connection to the local Station. In addition, there was an emergency vehicle, equipped with local and force radio, crewed by two officers and given all emergency calls. The Inspector agreed that I was to be a permanent emergency vehicle crew member with immediate effect. Delighted with this vote of confidence I found renewed enthusiasm for my work, and looking back, the next few months were the happiest of my career.

I was always an advocate of double-crewed police patrols. The driver could concentrate on the road while the passenger looked out for work. If one of us was feeling low or off colour the other one was there to encourage them. If there was trouble, especially if it was sudden, there was more chance of a message being put out for assistance. In violent situations, it was very reassuring to know that someone was watching your back, and apart from all that I enjoyed the company. In my time in the emergency vehicle, we had plenty of good calls to deal with, seeking out crime at night, and rushing from call to call during the day shifts. Some of the calls that we dealt with are related over the next chapter or two.

On my return to the section, I had more time to resume my participation in tug-of-war. Sgt Frank ran the team; we trained weekly at a local army base and were a pretty good little team. At the army base, we had a tripod made of street lamp standards, a pulley system extending over the top of the tripod with a rope attached to a large square heavy metal bucket. It was difficult enough to pull up the bucket when it was empty, but when it was loaded with rocks it presented a real challenge. Sgt Frank would train us and occasionally pull with us but he had a problem with a hernia. He would call stop, get off the rope, push the hernia back into his abdomen and resume his place on the rope!

A good number of the section were in the team, we trained when we were off duty and on, if we could get away with it. We were a light team coming in at a total of 108 stones. Whenever we could at weekends, we entered for competitions all over the area and often found ourselves matched against much bigger teams. Nevertheless, we often won, because we pulled as a team, eight men pulling as one. The prize was something like a barrel of beer and it made a good day out. We entered the Larkshire championship and reached the final. We lost in a very tough match by two ends to one to a team from deepest Larkshire. This team went on to win the national and then the world championship, so there was no disgrace in losing to them!

When involved in tug-of-war, police work was the furthest thing from our minds although all the other teams knew we were police. We were at a big competition in a nearby town when trouble broke out in the club bar and a fight developed involving several men. We were called into service and 10 of us trotted into the club, clad in our tug-of-war jerseys and wearing big hobnail boots. We seemed to strike fear into the hearts of the men fighting, it was very quickly ended, and the men dispersed. Shame we couldn't do that more often in the town centre on a Saturday night! We used that incident to demonstrate how useful our tug-of-war could be, and it certainly helped with our fitness, strength and comradeship, all-important parts of an effective police service.

At that time there were a great deal of sporting opportunities. The Force was very good in encouraging involvement and allowing time off for participation. The benefits of the training, the sustained fitness, the comradeship and teamwork and of course the kudos, for us and for the Force, if we did well, were recognised. I believe that is no longer the case and sporting involvement is no longer encouraged or supported. I understand the reasoning behind the shift in policy, but can't help feeling that it's rather a shame that a reasonable balance couldn't be achieved.

As a Police Force, we often found ourselves in conflict with another group who stuck together and drew strength from their relationship and that was gypsies, travellers, or pikies, as we tended to call them. Larkshire probably had more travellers than any other county in England. Many of them were domesticated, but scattered around Brightstone were a number of gypsy encampments. They were all places where police officers could expect to be greeted with great suspicion and hostility. One in particular became a no go area, because of the violent confrontations that occurred there. As a result, the Superintendent would not let us go without authorisation and sufficient manpower. In fact, on the last occasion I attended this site, when we were intent on making a number of arrests, there were 125 of us, including dog handlers and armed officers. And believe it or believe it not, our suspects were out!

Clearly many, and quite probably the majority, of gypsies were law abiding and caused their neighbours and the police no problems. However, there were a number who lived by petty crime and in addition a hard core of professional villains. These men were career criminals, men who were likely to be violent and dangerous to anyone who crossed them. They were brought up on fighting. For some of them a good night out was a few pints and a punch up to finish. Their upbringing and enjoyment of fighting made them very difficult people to deal with.

I had been sent on a plan-drawing course and was expected to provide accurate scale plans for court if they were needed. My services were called for at a rural pub. When I attended, I found that the place was completely wrecked. One evening some travellers were drinking in the pub and got drunk, foul mouthed and badly behaved. The Landlord told them to leave, they refused. So the Landlord and some of his regulars threw them out. Within an hour they were back with another group of travellers. They broke all the windows, smashed all the optics, broke up furniture and gave anyone who crossed them a savage beating. They came from a nearby gypsy encampment. Police Officers had attended and managed to arrest some of them who were charged with serious offences and were to appear at Crown Court. A scale plan was required which I duly provided. It wasn't very good and I was never asked again.

A dispute arose in a town centre pub one night between local men and a group of travellers. A brief confrontation broke out before the staff managed to stop it. The matter seemed to be resolved but when the four men involved left the pub their adversaries were waiting for them. Several travellers attacked them and beat them within an inch of their lives. There were several broken bones, extensive cuts, bruising, and a fractured skull, which needed a metal plate in a delicate and dangerous operation. The metal plate will be a life long reminder of that particular confrontation.

One traveller family in particular were active and very violent criminals, famed throughout a good part of the county and looked up to by many of the petty criminals of the area. As a result, we were frequently threatened by criminals who claimed they

166

were bosom buddies of this family. They were the core of the group police had tried to arrest in the violent confrontation that I mentioned earlier, which led to Sgt Frank giving evidence of his truncheon wielding at Crown Court. It was to their caravan that 125 of us went on an abortive attempt to arrest them.

The nearest police house to the site where they lived was usually empty, police officers and their families had lived there, but been driven out by broken windows, threats and attacks from these travellers. On the site, a klaxon had been set up and would be sounded if police attended, whereupon a large hostile crowd would quickly gather. It was a brave, or foolish, officer who went on the site at night. One officer did just that pursuing a stolen car. Once on the site a man emerged from the shadows and fired a shotgun into the police car. Another officer in similar circumstances was attacked and permanently blinded in one eye. Dogs were not as effective as usual. In one incident, a dog was set on some of these men; one of them caught the dog and threw it over a car before attacking the handler. The handler was so physically and mentally damaged by the incident that he had to retire on ill health. Another dog handler was a big powerful man, arguably the toughest and strongest officer, certainly in West Larkshire, probably in the whole county. Following an incident, he fought the smallest of this traveller family. He eventually overcame the man, but only after the toughest fight of his life. Perhaps the Superintendent was right in banning us from the site without proper authorisation, rankle as it did.

This family practiced intimidation against all who crossed them, including the police. When they were in court, members of the family would look for opportunities to threaten, for example, an officer using the gents might find a traveller next to him taking note of his shoulder number and promising to get him for giving evidence against them. On one occasion, I knew there were warrants out for arguably the toughest of these brothers. I saw him in the town and plucking up my courage arrested him. To my surprise and relief, he came quietly. In the Station, I asked him for his details to complete a charge sheet. He provided his name and address and then I asked him what his occupation was and he replied, 'Successful fucking thief!' He asked how much was outstanding on the warrants, produced a large wad of money, and paid them all off there and then in cash. I went on to serve him with summonses for various road traffic offences. 'You know what these mean, don't you?' No, what does it mean?' 'They mean that I will be disqualified from driving, still it's no skin off my nose, cos if I'm driving and you stand in my way boy, I'll fucking run yer down!'

Their occupation, as the one I had arrested told me, was theft, and thefts that varied from very professional jobs to burglaries that lacked any finesse. For example, there were a series of burglaries from garages. The modus operandi was to smash their way in, put a rope or a chain round the safe and yank it out of the floor and through any parts of the building that obstructed them. They could then take the safe back to the site and break in at their leisure. It was decided to carry out observations on rural garages in an attempt to catch them. Sure enough, they attacked one of the garages under observation. The officers attempted to arrest them, they didn't come quietly and I'm told it was quite a sight as the man I had arrested tried to make off, despite a number of officers clinging to him! He was eventually taken in, charged and later appeared at Crown Court. Despite being caught in the act, they pleaded not guilty and refused to admit breaking into any other garage. They were convicted and sent to prison for something like one year. I'm told they were model prisoners while inside, the only pity was that they couldn't be kept in for longer, much longer!

At the PC level, there was discussion about fighting fire with fire, i.e. dressing in civvies, wearing masks, arming ourselves with baseball bats or the like and going to the site and sorting them out. A couple of officers were really all for it, and it was quite seriously discussed. It was a dream of course, but it was a good dream! One officer really hated them as the result of his dealings with them. One day he was in the Station when he saw one of the brothers who had just been arrested. The PC leapt on him, knocked him down and tried to strangle him. Other officers had to, reluctantly, pull him off. There was just one officer that they seemed to respect and he also earned our respect by being prepared to go to the site and talk to them. Unfortunately, it wasn't possible to build on this relationship and extend it to the rest of us.

As we had found on some of the estates, the trouble with feuds like this one between police and members of the travelling community is that it spreads; it's all too easy for all travellers to come to hate police, and for police to come to hate all travellers. I'm not sure what the answer is, for there is a real conflict in the way we look at life. They had no respect for law, wanted to drive whatever they like, irrespective of the vehicles condition, or theirs! Driving licences, insurance, road tax or MOT certificates, what are they? They possessed illicit firearms, usually shotguns, and fights between them could be savage. They stole from and conned non-gypsies, in their mind - the rich, and that was perfectly ok in their view. Old people were often preyed on, colossal sums charged for a new drive, some gardening or even shear sharpening. Many of them claimed they didn't know their age or birthday and of course, many of them had no fixed address, which made taking action against them extremely difficult.

I'm sure they were kind to their families and to their friends, and I'm equally sure that if it were possible to sit down and talk with them they would have a very different view; not only of life, but also of the way police had treated them. Unfortunately, when people are speaking almost a different language, supported by very different understandings of the world, it is almost impossible to reach an accommodation. I became friendly with some travellers and asked them how we could reach them generally. They told me that I couldn't, it was completely impossible. Travellers will always have an us-and-them mentality and remain suspicious of all non-gypsies; I believe they called us goujas (spelt phonetically).

There were other groups who gathered together to support each other against the police, I have mentioned Hells Angels before. Then there were those who were close neighbours in various part of the town. There were a couple of estates where a good number of active criminals and trouble makers lived, and any opportunity to support one another against the police was not to be missed. The threat they sought to pose was often worse than the reality. When I was first patrolling one of the troublesome areas, I was threatened with the local 'boot boys'. In a group, they were brave enough, but alone, they were ineffective and cowardly as so many bullies are.

In my CID days, Tim and I attended a call in this area. When we came out of the house, a group of them were waiting for us with one sitting on the bonnet of the police car. They started to threaten us, but didn't get far before Tim knocked the youth off the car, and we manhandled the nearest youths out of the way. They immediately retreated, full of brave threats that were never backed up by actions.

Near the town centre was a close containing a number of five storey council flats. This close was a particular site of trouble. For example, I went there to serve a summons on a man living in a top floor flat. I duly served the summons on him as he stood at the door, whereupon he stood out on the landing shouting, 'witnesses, witnesses,' and tore up the summons, clearly intending to deny that it had ever been served. Others came out of their flats and were hostile and aggressive. Calmly and coolly, I walked through them and retired from the scene, trying hard not to show any of my inner concern!

One evening diners were enjoying an Indian meal in a restaurant just around the corner from this close. Two men were sitting at a table near the window drinking their first course of soup, when half a house brick came flying through the window and landed in their soup. For some reason or other, they took umbrage at this! They rushed out into the street and chased two men they saw running away. The men ran into the close, up the stairs and disappeared into a top floor flat. The two aggrieved diners continued their chase, kicked in the front door of the flat and found themselves confronted by the men they had chased, both now armed with large kitchen knives! They decided that it was time to call the cavalry and rang 999.

I was driving the emergency vehicle and responded to their call; I was accompanied by a young officer about to undergo a harsh lesson in some of the dangers of our profession. We met the men whose meal had been so rudely interrupted, and went with them to the flat. Having heard the story, we knocked on the door, but there was no reply. The complainants had broken the door lock, leaving the flat insecure, so we pushed the door open and went inside. We found ourselves confronted with the two suspects both wielding large kitchen knives. They had obviously been drinking and were not open to reason, although I tried hard to persuade them to give themselves up, pointing out that they were in enough trouble already. They would have none of it and moved forward to attack us with the knives.

We rapidly retired and pulled the door shut on them before calling for assistance.

Before too long other officers arrived including the duty Inspector. We tried again to persuade the suspects to give themselves up but their only response was abuse and threats. Then one of them saw the uniform of the Inspector and said that they were prepared to talk to the Inspector but no one else. They invited him to come alone into the flat to talk and he agreed, while whispering to us, 'there's no way I'm going in there alone, as soon as they open the door, rush them.' The modern police service has protective clothing, helmets and shields, we had none of those. We armed ourselves with our truncheons and one of us had a dustbin lid as a shield. When the door opened, we took our lives in our hands and rushed in. At the same time, other officers broke into the flat through a bedroom window and came round behind them. I managed to grab the knife arm of the nearest man and a colleague did likewise with the other man. After a short and violent struggle, they were overpowered and subdued without any of us being injured by the knives. We handcuffed them and dragged them out, still struggling violently, cursing, and swearing.

As we looked down into the courtyard, we saw that a hostile crowd of some 40 or 50 people had been drawn by the commotion and were now waiting at the bottom of the stairs and standing around the police cars. There was no other way out so we had little choice but to go down to the cars and try to negotiate whatever problems awaited us. We dragged the men to the stairs and on down as they continued to struggle and now call for help as they saw the crowd, while continuing to curse and threaten. The crowd were shouting at us to release their friends but taking no other action. As time progressed, they became more threatening and abusive. Going down a narrow staircase meant that only two men could be abreast so manhandling them down was no easy task. I was with the first man, pushing him down in front of me and holding on to him with the handcuffs, which held his hands securely behind his back. As we neared the bottom of the stairs, he lost his balance and fell forward. I couldn't hold him and he fell forward down the last few steps. With his hands handcuffed behind his back, he was unable to protect himself and landed heavily on his face. Inevitably, he suffered facial injuries, which didn't seem to knock any sense into him, and bled from his wounds. The incident inflamed the crowd who became even more vociferous and threatening.

Other officers joined us and we moved the men through the hostile crowd to the police cars and opened the nearest car door ready to put them inside. One of the nearest men in the crowd took the opportunity to kick the car door shut. This was the catalyst for a general attack on us and an attempt to release their mates. We had to fight our way out of the close. We held on doggedly to our prisoners, but were forced to abandon our police vehicles, which were already suffering heavy damage. Other cars came and we took the suspects to the Police Station.

A little later, a force of officers returned to the close to recover the cars. The crowd had dispersed by then but the police vehicles had been extensively damaged, all the windows broken, the blue lights knocked off and dents in most if not all the body panels and all the tyres slashed. The cars were taken back to the Station by local garages and the officers dispersed to their normal duties leaving my young colleague and me to process our prisoners. That should have been the end of the incident but it proved to be far from it.

As we continued with our work, we heard a commotion from the front office, the public counter of the Police Station. I went to see what was going on and found a large number of people from the close, jammed into the small public area, threatening the Station Sergeant and demanding the release of their friends. The Station Sergeant gave them short shrift and told them to clear off, whereupon one of the men leaned across the counter and punched the Sergeant in the face. The Sergeant was having none of that and he went up and over the counter after his assailant. The group all gathered round him and he literally disappeared from view! Turning to the white faced and very shocked civilian woman telephonist, I told her to call for assistance, and I went over the counter to help the Sergeant. A very violent fight ensued as he and I fought against considerable odds for some minutes. In the confined space only three or four assailants could reach us at one time, and in our initial response we threw a few out of the Station, but the others pushed forward, driving us back against the door to the inside of the Station. Our desperate struggle continued for some minutes until other officers arrived and helped us to throw the lot out of the Police Station. I freely admit, kicking, punching, elbowing and manhandling anyone, man or woman, within range during this violent confrontation, when we were being punched, kicked and otherwise physically mistreated.

The crowd remained outside the Police Station shouting, swearing, and demanding to see a senior officer to complain about our police brutality! To my amazement and dismay, the duty Inspector, who although he had been in the Station, had turned up too late to help in ejecting them, decided to allow a deputation in to make their complaints. I told him that this was not the right course of action. They should all be arrested, locked up for the night and charged with criminal damage to the police vehicles, assault, breach of the peace and causing an affray. The Inspector wouldn't agree and insisted that no arrests be made and he would listen to their complaints. I wish we had found the opportunity to arrest the lot of them before he arrived on the scene, and I won't tell you what I thought of his decision.

A deputation from this rabble was duly allowed in and the Inspector recorded their complaint. They then dispersed feeling that, on the whole, the day had been theirs, they had inflicted more damage and humiliation on us than they had sustained. However, they didn't secure the release of their friends and these two remained in custody until they appeared before the Magistrates Court. The Sergeant and I had a few bumps and bruises but no injuries of any consequence.

Following up of their complaints could not take place until after the court case. Thankfully, the subsequent investigation of their allegations led to the decision that our actions were justifiable, I should think so too! The duty Inspector and CID officers considered what actions should be taken against other offenders. Despite my hopes and pleas, it was decided not to pursue action against any other offenders, apart from the original two. The moment had passed, if we had arrested them on the night we could identify them, but the next day we would be unable to point out hardly any of them. So the men and women who had damaged police cars, punched and kicked police officers and done their best to prevent us carrying out lawful arrests were let off scot-free! The original two men were charged with criminal damage; assault and resisting arrest and eventually found themselves appearing at Crown Court.

They pleaded not guilty and many of their neighbours were called as witnesses. One or two claimed to have seen more than they did, but most of them focussed on the incident from the time of their neighbour's arrest, alleging police brutality. One after another, they stood up to condemn the police, alleged that I had thrown one of the prisoners down the stairs, and admitted kicking and punching officers, smashing police car windows and the like. They were each asked what action had been taken against them and each said none. The defence were cleverly putting in the Jury's mind the thought that the police hadn't proceeded against all these people because they had something to hide, or knew that they were in the wrong. I don't mind admitting that my blood boiled as I listened to all this. Thankfully guilty verdicts were eventually returned on the two, and they were sent to prison for 18 months. A good result at last, at least against those two. The others dispersed scowling and cursing at us.

Some of the residents of this close continued to cause problems for both the police and the public until the whole close was demolished a couple of years later and all the residents dispersed round the other council estates in the town. It is a difficult problem for councils to decide what to do with troublesome families. Should they put them all together and form a kind of ghetto, or should they disperse them as widely as possible in the hope that responsible neighbours will have a positive influence on them? There are arguments for both policies within council circles and within police circles. I promised that I wouldn't be pontificating on society's problems so I leave the solutions to others.

Police inevitably work closely with the other emergency services especially the Ambulance and the Fire Service. We got on very well with the Ambulance Brigade, their Station was a good tea-stop, we exchanged friendly words whenever we met and in the course of duty, we were often so relieved to see an Ambulance crew. In most cases, we would be on the scene of any incident before the Ambulance. We were all trained in First Aid and held certificates, but most of us had to admit that it was a pretty rudimentary knowledge and although we did our best, many cases were beyond our capabilities and equipment. I related the first fatal accident that I attended, when I was so grateful to a nurse and then to the ambulance crew and there were many such incidents. I remember a car accident, which left a man trapped in the driver's seat caught by his foot and lower leg, which had been partially severed. He was in terrible pain, which we could do nothing to alleviate. It was a great relief when the ambulance crew arrived. It was 40 minutes before the Fire Brigade could release the driver; the ambulance crew were able to ease his pain with oxygen and call a Doctor to give him a pain killing injection. That scenario was repeated time and time again in one form or another.

For some reason we did not have the same relationship with the Fire Service. I tried, we all tried to be friendly and to get on well, but it just didn't seem to happen. We were polite enough but there was no warmth, and I was never invited to have a cup of tea at the Fire Station. I don't know it they were suspicious of us or there was some other problem that we never got to the bottom of. I have a great respect for the work they do and the bravery they show, although the damage they sometimes cause is difficult to justify. I went once to a call about a house on fire. I arrived before the Fire Service, found the front door locked and no answer to my knocking, so I went round the back and was able to go in through the unlocked back door. I couldn't get upstairs because of the smoke but was able to check the ground floor. The Fire Service arrived, found the front door locked, so out came the axes and the door was smashed down! I guess we all do things the hard way sometimes when with a little thought there is an easier way.

When the Firemen went on strike, we were asked to help the Green Goddess crews as much as possible, they often didn't know the area and had difficulty finding the nearest water. On the first day of the strike, I was out on mobile patrol when I saw some smoke coming from a house. I knocked on the door but there was no reply, and the rest of the house was secure, so I forced the door open to find the place well alight and unoccupied. I called for a fire crew and tried to use the cars fire extinguisher, which, perhaps unsurprisingly, had no effect. A Green Goddess duly turned up and the crew tackled the fire, in what seemed to me a professional manner. A little crowd gathered outside and among them was a teenage girl who I had seen in the area when I first arrived. I went over to talk to her and she was evasive and avoided eye contact. I took her with me as I talked to the fire crew and they were of the opinion that the fire had been started deliberately. I arrested the girl and took her back to the Station where she eventually admitted that she had started the fire because she wanted to see a Green Goddess in action! So I had the distinction of attending the first fire after the strike started and making an arrest. A good morning's work.

Chapter 12 Death

As I have mentioned before, it is part of a Policeman's lot to deal with death in its many forms. As a section, we had lost Peter in a motorcycle accident and we were to lose another young colleague. Derek was just 26 years old, keen and smart, building a promising career and getting on well with all of us. He was fit, active, and played football. On one early shift, he was on mobile patrol with a colleague when he collapsed. He was taken to hospital where they carried out a number of tests before discharging him as fit and well. The following weekend he went to stay with his parents, along with his wife and young son. He suddenly collapsed and died in front of them all, despite his wife's valiant efforts to revive him. It must have been such a terrible shock. The cause of death was a virus of the heart, which, it was claimed, was undetectable when the tests were carried out just a few days earlier.

Another sad funeral with a police honour guard and a very full chapel, our hearts going out to his wife and child, and all the family. Although many of us thought that we had become used to death, it hits so much harder when it is someone close to you. It's easy to think that in each case we dealt with, we empathised with the bereaved, and we did to the best of our ability, but fortunately, it didn't touch us in quite the same way.

Death in some of its more ugly forms was very difficult to deal with. It was one thing to deal with the sudden death of an elderly person, or even a fatal accident involving someone of very mature years, but a very different matter if it was a child. Some of the terrible things that happened could reduce the strongest man to tears. The sight of a child on the morticians slab was so poignant and so wrong. I always found it quite shocking to look at young smooth skin on the face and body of a dead child, laying there almost peacefully, and yet the cause of so much pain and lack of peace. I was much more used to the `lived in frame` we all develop with the passing of the years.

Thankfully, I never had to attend a fatal road accident where children were killed, but many of my colleagues did. I remember only too well some of their terrible tales; of the mangled body of a child trapped under a lorry's wheels, or a high speed crash where a young girl's leg was ripped off and lay by the side of the road. We all tried to develop coping strategies, many, perhaps the majority of officers, tried to become so hardened that they didn't feel the pain, or enter into the horror of the scene. However when it was a child, the tough veneer was torn away and the reality they faced hurt deeply and threatened to overwhelm defences. 'Men don't cry,' is a fallacy, but is nevertheless perpetuated by many police officers. I didn't want to become hardened by death, nor did I want to be overcome by sadness or grief. I hoped to be able to go through all the feelings, rather than round them, and to carry out my duties as sympathetically as possible.

I was at the mortuary one day as the Pathologist was busy conducting post mortems. The first one was a man in his early 70's who had collapsed and died suddenly, it was believed from a heart attack. The heart was indeed the cause of his death, with part of the heart wall as thin as paper. As the Pathologist was dissecting the lungs, he spotted some congestion. 'This man has a cancer,' he exclaimed, and embarked on a search for it. There was nothing in the organs usually removed, so he continued the search. Eventually he found a small tumour in the lower bowel. 'That would have killed him in time' he told us. I couldn't help but be impressed by his skill. As he cut out the kidneys and passed them to the Mortician to weigh them, the Mortician looked at them and observed, 'I've got kidneys for dinner tonight.' I think that put me off kidneys for life!

The Pathologist went on to work on a much younger man who had committed suicide. He asked if we knew why, he was told that the man had a number of problems, among them was his belief that he had cancer of the testicles. With one swift stroke of his scalpel, the Pathologist removed the testicles, cut them open and pronounced, 'No, he didn't,' before throwing the testicles into the man's stomach cavity and carrying on with his grisly work! I'm not criticising the Pathologist or Mortician in any way, but there is a danger of falling into the trap of proving the truth of that old saying, 'familiarity breeds contempt'.

Most of the sudden deaths that we attended were fairly straightforward and involved elderly people living alone. I do not intend any disrespect, but I have to admit that as time passes it is difficult to remember them all. Most of these deaths were of people I never met in life and encountered only in death. Their relatives too I only met in their shock and grief. I do remember some of the times waiting in the Mortuary for a post mortem to be carried out, or to carry out the identification of a body. Especially I remember times when I was there alone, when there were a number of bodies waiting for attention. Sometimes my imagination made me think one of them moved. I believe it's true that men's facial hair can continue to grow after death. I recall one young man, around 30 years, killed by an asthma attack, lying on that cold slab with stubble on his face looking as if it still grew as he slept.

Although the passing years have erased the memories of many of the sudden deaths I attended, there were others that have remained with me always. A young woman woke up one morning to find her 33 year old husband dead next to her. We learned later that he had suffered a brain haemorrhage and died early in the night. By the time she woke and realised that he was dead he was cold and rigor mortis had set in, together with the familiar skin discolouration where all the blood settles at the bottom of the body. What could anyone say to bring that poor woman some comfort? I dealt with it as best as I could and then had to leave her in the charge of her family.

On occasions, I had to attend cot deaths, far too many I'm afraid. I was almost overwhelmed by the terrible tragedy of it all as I stood with grieving parents looking at that tiny still frame, or tried to gently remove the baby from mother's desperate embrace. In one case, the baby had died with his face against the bars of the cot, which had squashed up his little features. The mother was so distressed at how ugly her son looked when he had been such a beautiful baby. The mere presence of police could be distressing, did we suspect foul play? We attended on behalf of the Coroner and made a report to him through the offices of the Coroners Officer, a senior PC.

I attended accidents where people had been burnt to death, killed by machinery in industrial accidents, suffocated by a plastic bag during a bizarre sexual experiment and of course killed in road traffic accidents, which could be truly horrific.

Then there were the deaths from suicide. Fume filled cars and drugs overdoses and even hangings were at least not too messy. Death by jumping in front of a train or from a bridge onto a motorway were terribly messy affairs and the poor drivers involved probably never quite recovered. The road or railway had to be closed while police tried to collect up the pieces of body which sometimes had been dragged for hundreds of yards. Thankfully, I avoided that task. An outline of the incident helped us to have an idea what to expect when attending such a scene, which gave us the opportunity to mentally prepare. A more common sight was people who had killed themselves with a firearm, usually a shotgun. I found that I could just about bear the sight of it if I had an idea what to expect, i.e. a neighbour had heard a shot or the deceased had rung a relative to tell them of his intentions. However, when there was no suggestion of violent death and the deceased was suddenly discovered, the full horror of the scene would make my stomach turn over.

I went to the home of a farmer who hadn't been seen around by neighbours for a while. After the usual unsuccessful enquiries, I broke in and found him lying dead. He was on his back on a bed, lying in a pool of blood having shot himself with a shotgun, which lay by his side. The force of the discharge had blown half his head off and scattered blood and brains on the floor and up the wall. He had left a note saying that he felt sorry for those of us who were left in this cruel, horrible world but he had had enough of it. I stood there for quite a while taking in this terrible scene and wondering how he had got into such a state of mind. I called a doctor and a funeral director and then found the phone number of his son. I rang him to ask him to come over, but not until we had removed the body. I felt so sorry for him with all that mess to clear up that I returned after work to help him burn the mattress and blankets and wash down the room. There is no mechanism for clearing up the scene of such a tragedy. It is down to the family.

We were obliged to call a doctor in every case of sudden death. Police officers are not qualified to say that someone is dead, no matter how obvious it is, it has to be a doctor. Sometimes we would call a police surgeon but often it was the local GP. It was clear that some of them were not used to violent or messy deaths and struggled to cope with the sight that confronted them.

One hot summer day we were called to a caravan located on the very edge of town. Inside we found the partially decomposed body of a man, infested with maggots and stinking to high heaven. We were still obliged to call a doctor and one duly arrived but wouldn't go into the caravan, he did go as far as looking through the window to confirm death. Who could blame him? When the body was moved, the outline of the body remained on the mattress, made by his body fats leeching into it. Funeral Directors were called and removed the body. If we had to move decomposing bodies, we could claim a special allowance of some £2.50. Surprisingly we didn't leap at the chance! The doctor of course, was paid considerably more than £2.50 for looking through the window and pronouncing death.

One of the most tragic deaths that I attended concerned two 12 year old boys. They had gone with their fathers on a shooting trip. The boys had remained by the car to play as their fathers went off. They had opened the car boot and discovered a 12 bore shotgun. Standing it up they looked at it and then one lad asked the other if it was loaded. The lad holding the gun said he would check, bent down and pulled the trigger. The gun was loaded, and the other lad was standing right over the barrel. The shotgun cartridge hit him half way up his face, split his head in two and hurled his brain some 30 feet up the field.

The other lad, terribly shocked and distressed, got a passing member of the public to call for help and we arrived before the fathers had returned to the scene. When they did arrive, we had to physically restrain the dead lad's father to stop him going to his boy and having to see those terrible injuries. I shall never forget the sight of that poor lad lying in a field, his young life torn away from him in such a tragic accident. I can't remember if any action was taken against the careless father, but maybe he had suffered enough. The incident was an awful reminder that firearms are dangerous and lethal.

Perhaps the worst sight that I ever saw started in the usual way, a neighbour reporting that the man next door hadn't been seen for a while. I gained admission and looked for him, ending up in the downstairs bedroom where I found myself confronted by a sight that at first I just couldn't make sense of. There was an awful smell, the window was covered with thousands of flies, the floor was awash with maggot-infested blood and other offensive semi congealed liquids and the man? There was something or someone against the bed but I couldn't quite work out what it was. Eventually I realised that it was a man with no legs, they had obviously both been amputated some time in the past, he was leaning over the bed towards a pot and his head had fallen into it.

Eventually it transpired that the poor chap kept a pot under the bed due to his lack of mobility. During the night, he had urinated and defecated in the pot. He then felt ill and had vomited into it. Probably as he was doing that an aneurysm high up in his aorta burst and his life blood poured out into the pot, as he died he fell headfirst into it, with the rest of his body vertical against the bed, and the whole mess in the pot had overflowed and poured out across the floor. What a dreadful, lonely death it must have been. How I managed not to be ill myself I really don't know.

I called a doctor and a firm of funeral directors and among the deceased's papers found the phone number of a district nurse who had been caring for him. I rang the nurse who attended promptly, took one look at the mess and said to me, 'leave it to me, I'll soon have this cleared up.' We got the man onto the bed, she wiped his face and as soon as his body had been removed, she set about cleaning the floor. I was very, very grateful to her and full of admiration for undertaking a task that I just don't think I could have faced.

Although I had been involved in enquiries following murders I hadn't actually attended a scene before the body was removed, or if I had, I had no reason to see the body in situ, the fewer people who invade the scene the better. However one evening I was called to an incident in a housing estate on the south side of town. In the upstairs bedrooms were two children who had been terribly battered about the head, one was dead with blood and brains splattered up the wall and even on the ceiling, the other child was alive, just. Downstairs in the lounge was a woman, dead from a shotgun blast. Her husband had found them and was naturally distraught. The sight was truly awful and even very experienced detectives looked decidedly green.

It seemed that the husband had gone out to get some cigarettes and his wife, who was also the children's mother, had snapped for some reason, attempted to kill her children and then shot herself. She hadn't been able to put the shotgun in her mouth and reach the trigger, so she had put the barrel up her nose and then fired. The shotgun was small calibre so she hadn't blown her head off, but it was still very messy with the back of her head blown out by the force of the shot.

When the living child had been conveyed to hospital, the body of the other child removed and the forensic examination of the scene concluded, it was decided to leave the mothers body in situ for a while pending further tests. I was given the task of remaining at the scene to preserve its integrity until the enquiry team returned, which was likely to be a few hours.

I wandered round the house for a while and then sat in the lounge in an armchair facing the dead woman, taking the opportunity to think about all that had happened and wonder what had led up to it, were there signs that should have been seen? Was there a lesson for us all to learn? Would we ever learn the full truth, which only she ultimately knew? After a while, my mind wandered away from deep questions and I couldn't help thinking what a nice suite it was and what a shame that she had ruined an armchair with her blood and brains.

I had some food with me for my break. As time went by, I became peckish, but hoped to be relieved so that I could go back to the Station to eat. Eventually hunger got the better of me and I got out my sandwiches and ate them as I sat opposite her. I certainly wouldn't have done that a few years ago, but now? How could I reconcile my actions with 'familiarity breeds contempt' that I worried about at the beginning of the chapter? Well I reasoned that she didn't mind, I was hungry and I was becoming more used to death in all its forms. I never became fully used to it, I didn't want to be, and I resolved to monitor myself to make sure that was the case.

In many ways having to tell people that a relative had died, was an even harder task than attending the scene of a death. People's reactions are so different; I related the story of the wife who attacked me. At the other extreme was a nurse who I saw at work in hospital. I took her into the sister's office and told her that her husband, who was only in his forty's, had collapsed and died at work. She thanked me politely for telling her and then said, 'if you'll excuse me, I must get back to work now!' I was very concerned for her and spoke to the ward sister, who promised that she would take care of her. On another occasion the relatives seemed to think that I had killed their loved one, and became extremely hostile, I retired quickly from the scene.

Over time, I came to see that it was usually unnecessary to say very much. A Policeman on the doorstep is nearly always the bringer of bad news. A suitably grave face and a request to come in, followed by the suggestion that they sit down, would almost inevitably lead to them asking me, 'is it George, not Vicky', etc and we took it from there. Sometimes I wished that we could occasionally deliver good news. Perhaps we could tell them when they had won the pools, or come up on premium bonds. At other times, as in delivering death messages, the expectation made the job easier.

Our normal procedure was to stay a while, and if we possibly could, determine if there was anyone we could ring to come and be with them, perhaps make a cup of tea and be reluctant to leave until they had someone with them. It was nearly always a woman that we had to break the bad news to and we sometimes used the services of a WPC. Often it was necessary to go on from delivering the bad news to ask who could identify the body, and take them to the mortuary for the task. I always found the whole job very draining and difficult. I never got used to the deaths and sadnesses we encountered and it gave me, and I'm sure many other colleagues, a frequent reminder of the fragility of life, which was in turn an encouragement to live it to the full while we could.

Chapter 13 Court appearances

Part of a Policeman's life is having to appear at court, hopefully as a witness! Attendance was usually at Magistrates Court but sometimes at Crown Court. It was always a slightly nerve-racking occasion, as one of my colleagues put it, 'the best laxative known to the police!' Generally, courts are sober and serious places and those officiating take themselves very seriously indeed, and woe betide anyone who offends the court, especially a Crown Court Judge. A man sitting in the public gallery, obviously bored with proceedings, got a newspaper out. The Judge had him brought before him, gave him a good telling off for his lack of respect, and threatened to send him to prison for contempt of court if he did it again!

A story is told which I have never been able to verify. At a nearby town, some eight miles away, there was an RAF airfield, long since built upon. Aircraft from there would fly over the court disrupting proceedings. A Judge sent a note to the senior officer of the airfield telling him not to fly over the court when it was in session. The RAF officer ignored the note and aircraft continued flying over the court. The Judge then issued a warrant for the arrest of the officer in charge and had him brought before him. 'You will not fly over my court when it is in session.' He never did it again. A great story, whether apocryphal or not, and it does demonstrate the power and attitude of senior Judges.

When the senior Judges, High Court Judges, came to Brightstone, they were greeted with great ceremony. There was a processional service in the big town church attended by the mayor and other dignitaries. The Judge was lodged at a large house just outside the town and guarded by armed police. He came to court in a chauffeur driven limousine with a police motorcycle escort. When he arrived, he was greeted by a number of police officers, all in best uniforms and white gloves, with an officer of at least Inspector rank to greet him. On their first visit there was even a fanfare, as he swept in, clad in wig and red robe. At lunchtime he went back to the house, all traffic lights on his route were turned to green for him, as his escorted limousine swept through the town.

Despite the solemnity of court proceedings there were occasional lighter moments. On one occasion, a German defendant appeared before the Magistrates Court. He pleaded that he couldn't speak English and the Chairman of the Bench asked if anyone in court could speak German. A member of the public who had done some of his national service in Germany volunteered. 'Ask him what is his name,' said the Chairman. 'Vot iz your name?' said the 'translator' to much laughter from sections of the court and much disapproval from the Bench!

An Inspector at Brightstone had his house burgled. In fairly short order the offenders were arrested and much of the property recovered, yes the police do succeed sometimes! Among the stolen property was a carton of 200 cigarettes. All the recovered property was evidence and was kept in a special property store in the Station. One day the Inspector wanted a cigarette and being short of money decided to take some of his own from the store, intending to replace them later. He repeated this several times until they were all gone. Eventually the case came to court and the property was required as evidence. On the morning of the case, the Inspector suddenly remembered that he had smoked all the cigarettes. He rushed round to the nearest newsagent and purchased 200 cigarettes of the same brand. In court he gave his evidence, as he did he kept thinking that he knew the Chairman of the Bench from somewhere but he couldn't quite place him. As he identified the cigarettes as the very same ones stolen from his house he suddenly realised who the Chairman was - the newsagent! The Chairman fixed him with a steely glare as the Inspectors knees trembled, but fortunately, he said nothing.

Some of the Judges were real characters. One particular High Court Judge noted for his brusque manner was presiding one day over a case involving buggery of rent boys. The defendant was duly convicted and the Judge said to him, 'stand up. You are a dirty little man doing dirty little things to dirty little boys, you will go to prison for four years, take him down.' A pearl of concise sentencing. On another occasion, he told a defence barrister that he had no defence apart from attacking the good name of police officers and he wasn't having that, as the barrister had nothing else to say he had better sit down. Wonderful stuff!

In the Magistrates Court, police officers often conducted the prosecutions; usually it was an Inspector or Sergeant. However if the need arose I had that privilege on several occasions as Acting Sergeant and thoroughly enjoyed it. They wouldn't let me loose on the more important cases, but I still had the occasional chance to cross-examine and cross swords with solicitors. Representation was normally carried out by solicitors. In the days before the Crown Prosecution Service, the police would sometimes use local solicitors as well. Some of them were very competent but it appeared many solicitors were not trained advocates and it showed. On occasion a barrister would appear, usually cultured, articulate and competent and sometimes seeming to hold the court in thrall with the power of their advocacy and sheer presence.

Among the ranks of barristers there were some very good ones and of course some rather inept ones. In the Crown Court, a wise Policeman didn't try to cross swords with them. They were on home ground, well used to the cut and thrust of examining witnesses, and generally better equipped in any verbal battle. One of them, a QC, was held in especially high esteem. I was told of one of his triumphs. He was defending a company against a claim for industrial injuries. The complainant had suffered a serious arm injury restricting his movement. The QC asked him if he could show the court his maximum movement up and down, and then from side to side, the complainant duly complied. 'Now will you show the court how far you could move your arm before the accident?' And he did!

I attended a call one night to a farm on the edge of town. A neighbour had rung in because the farmer's dogs were all barking, and despite the lights being on he could get no answer on the telephone. I found the farmhouse completely insecure at the front and back. The front door was actually wide open. All the lights were on, but there was no sign of anyone. I had a look around inside and outside without success. There was no sign of a break in, or anything suspicious. I found an address book and rang a few numbers. I spoke to a couple of the farmers friends, who told me that he often left the house like that when he went out! As I looked round, I came across a double-barrelled shotgun and then a .22 rifle. Neither of them was secured in any way. The rifle should have been in a secure cabinet. Ammunition for both weapons was scattered all over the place, by the bed, alongside the kitchen sink, and in an ashtray in the lounge. I confiscated the weapons and the ammunition and left a note giving my details and explaining what I had done and why.

The following day the farmer rang in before I came on duty. I later returned the call and told him I was going to retain his weapons and submit a report questioning his suitability for firearm and shotgun certificates. He was none to pleased and explained how he needed them, but I felt that action needed to be taken, especially in view of his friend's comments, so his plea fell on deaf ears. I submitted a report, which found its way to an Assistant Chief Constable, who decided to withdraw both his firearm and shotgun certificates. When that happens there is a right of appeal to a Crown Court Judge, and the farmer exercised that right.

Before too long I found myself at Crown court with the ACC. I didn't often mix with ACC's and was a little bit nervous. However, he was a lovely chap, who put me at my ease. I gave my evidence first and then waited for the farmers counsel to cross-examine. 'Officer, have you ever made a mistake?' 'Yes, sir.' 'And when you make a mistake do you hope to find forgiveness and understanding, or is it right for one mistake to merit unforgiving punishment?' 'I would hope for forgiveness, sir.' 'Then why didn't you practice forgiveness with my client for one isolated mistake?' 'I don't believe it was an isolated mistake.' 'How do you know it wasn't an isolated mistake?' 'Well, I found an address book and rang some of your client's friends; they told me that it was a regular occurrence.' 'Were they friends, they could have been hostile or even joking with you, couldn't they?' 'That's true, sir?' 'So on the basis of unsubstantiated reports from people you didn't know, who may or may not be friends, you have deprived my client of much needed tools of his trade. Yes or no?' 'No, sir.' 'What do you mean, no, that is exactly what happened it is not?' 'Well, sir...' 'Yes or no, officer?' I tried to explain but he cut me short. 'Yes or no, officer?'

I turned to the Judge and asked if I could explain, he overruled counsels objection and allowed my explanation. 'Setting aside the house's insecurity, and how many times that may or may not have happened, the shotgun should have been secured, and it was not. The rifle should have been in a secure cabinet, and it was not. The ammunition should also have been in a secure cabinet, it was not. In fact the ammunition was carelessly left lying around in at least three different locations.' 'Thank you, Officer.' Turning to counsel, 'have you any further questions?' 'No further questions, your honour.' Good old Sergeant Frank, what would I do without his example.

I sat in the well of the court as the ACC gave his evidence. He was questioned closely about the Force Policy, which he explained with clarity and authority. I couldn't help noticing they were all more respectful to him than to me, but such is life. At the end the Judge ruled that I had done the right thing, and the ACC had correctly supported my decision. However, the weapons were tools of the appellant's trade and so his firearms should be restored to him in 30 days and his certificates were to remain valid. Was it all worth the effort I wondered, the case must have cost a small fortune and the only ones who really benefit are the lawyers. Still, I hope the farmer had learned a lesson, and the ACC said he was impressed with my evidence.

When I was a young PC, I made a terrible mistake that could have cost me dearly. I was on Crown Court duty, there to prevent any problems, safeguard the Judge etc. There was a big case in progress with HM customs prosecuting some major drug smugglers. Customs officers were giving evidence and as the rules dictate, the witnesses go into court one at a time and should not speak to each other in between one giving their evidence and the next one going in. The court rose for lunch while one customs officer was still giving evidence.

I was standing in the hall outside court when a customs officer approached me, handed me a note and asked me to give it to a colleague for him. Without thinking, I agreed and walked to the witness room, met the other officer on the way and gave him the note. As I did so, the court door was open and I noticed one of the defence barristers staring at me intently. He then wrote something on a piece of paper in front of him. I suddenly realised that the man who had given me the note was the officer giving evidence and the one I had given the note to was almost certainly the next one in. I was absolutely horrified at what I'd done and the possible implications. If the barrister reported me, I was in danger of being prosecuted for attempting to pervert the course of justice and I could face a prison sentence. Saying there was no criminal intent and I just didn't think would cut no ice.

I didn't know what to do, I couldn't think of anything I could do, except hope that the barrister took no action. I was back in court in the afternoon on real tenterhooks that this barrister would take some action. In the event, the barrister had no opportunity to say anything, but would he go and see the Judge afterwards? Would he write a complaint? Court rose for the weekend and we all went home. I told my wife what had happened and the possible consequences, and we spent a very fraught weekend worrying about what might happen. On Monday I was back in court as the case continued, I held my breath when the barrister in question stood up to talk, but he made no mention of what he had seen. As the trial continued I began to relax a little, the more time that passed, the less likely it was that he had reported me. Eventually the trial came to its conclusion and the barristers made their closing addresses. I felt really tense again, it was his last chance to say something in open court, unless he was waiting to see what the verdict was, and if it went against his client bring up the matter then!

The jury retired and I suspect I was nearly as nervous as the defendants as we waited for the verdict. After some hours, they returned to bring in a guilty verdict. Each barrister then stood to make representation on behalf of his client to try to mitigate their sentence. Finally, it came to my barrister and my heart was in my mouth as he stood. Again, he made no mention of my actions, sentence was passed, and the trial came to its conclusion. I went and stood where the barristers would pass me as they left in order that he could speak to me if he wanted to. It seemed to take ages before he came out. As he passed me, he gave me an intense look, but said nothing as he left the building. Why he didn't report me, I'll never know. He clearly saw me and wrote something, but I never knew what was in the note. How could I have been so stupid? The incident reminded me how just one moment's foolishness could ruin a career, and how important it is when on duty to concentrate all the time, and examine my actions before I take them, difficult as that sometimes was.

A real problem for the police was, and still is, the necessity of having to make instant decisions that are then examined and dissected at leisure. People who were drunk, dishevelled and violent at night become sober suited, polite citizens when they appeared in court in the morning to deny that they could ever have done the things alleged against them.

One night I was on patrol with Rob, I was driving as we went down some quiet side roads. It was around 0300 and as we came to the end of a cul-de-sac, we saw four youths walking along. I pulled up alongside them and Rob asked them where they were going at that time of night. 'Fuck-all to do with you copper,' came the reply. Rob wasn't one to let that go by, he got out, stood in front of them and said, 'I'll ask you again, where are you going at this time of night?' 'You mind your own fucking business and we'll mind ours,' the same one replied. By now, I had joined Rob and we physically stopped them by standing in front of them. We told them in no uncertain terms, that if they wouldn't answer our questions, they would give rise to suspicion that they had or were about to commit crime and we were going to detain and search them. In response, the mouthy one threw a punch at Rob and in an instant we were involved in a fight, outnumbered two to one. I managed to call for assistance as we struggled to subdue them until help arrived. Within a few minutes colleagues were on the scene and they were overpowered and arrested.

They were uninjured and we had only suffered a few cuts and bruises. Although they were minor, we had to go to the police surgeon for a report to be drawn up describing our injuries. Other officers interviewed the youths while we were being treated. Eventually the youths came up with an explanation for their presence in the road at that time; they had nothing criminal on them and no record. If they were up to no good, we couldn't prove it. They were charged with assault on police and a breach of the peace. When they appeared before the magistrate's court a few days later they were transformed into spruced up, polite young men, who had been unjustly picked on by rude aggressive Policemen. Them swear at the police or refuse to cooperate? Never! Fortunately, the commotion that night had woken a nearby householder who had seen what happened from his bedroom window and gave evidence on our behalf. We gave our evidence and the magistrates retired to consider their verdict, always a worrying time. Eventually they returned and convicted them. Their sentence was a short community service order, in view of them being nice young men, never in trouble before, contrite good citizens who had a misunderstanding with police!

We couldn't help wondering what the sentence might have been if the bench had been in our shoes that night, it is too easy to sanitise it all. We tried to do our job, and the circumstances demanded that we made an instant decision whether to let them go or take action. They appeared not to have done anything, but what were they doing there, far from home, at that time of night and why be so aggressive? Once the fight started, we didn't know if they had weapons, they hit Rob first; we were outnumbered and could have got a good hiding. What price punching a copper in the face without reason? A few hours' community service, little wonder some officers were disillusioned with courts and some others were all for dishing out their own justice, especially in such cases.

I did try to put myself in the shoes of Magistrates and Judges, well-intentioned people, who generally speaking hadn't seen the side of life we daily met. It must be difficult when looking at smart, presentable and polite young men, to imagine them as we saw them. Sometimes the defendants just couldn't believe themselves what they had done. Due to drink or drugs, they had no recollection of the previous night and indeed, they were very different people in the morning. It's probably true that we in the police hoped and perhaps half expected the courts to believe and trust us, and to convict and sentence, as we would like. Sadly, some police do tell lies, which damages all of us. Clearly the courts have to be even handed, and it is also true that most of us police officers were politically a little to the right of Attila the Hun, believing in capital punishment, flogging and hard labour without remission! To us, assault on police demanded and deserved a stiff prison sentence, and we felt aggrieved that offenders seemed to be given shorter sentences for assaulting police than assaulting other members of the public, as if it's part of the job for us to get the odd punch or kick.

Compare that with the dignity of the court, where assaulting a Policeman got a non custodial slap on the wrist, while reading a newspaper in court very nearly earned seven days in prison! The following indicates the court's opinion of it's own importance. Over the years many excuses have been offered for speeding, the vast majority of them fall on deaf ears, imminent birth or death might do it but little else. A Policeman was convicted of speeding, fined and his licence endorsed. He appealed to the Crown Court; his grounds were that he was speeding so that he wouldn't be late for a Crown Court case. Appeal upheld! Enough pontificating. Time to move on.

The little girl next door knocked on my door one day to tell me that she had found a small dog. I drove her down to the Police Station to hand it in. On the way, I saw a car with five youths in it, always worth a look, and as I did, I recognised the young man driving as a disqualified driver. With the little girl and being off duty, I was severely handicapped in trying to take any immediate action. We stopped at traffic lights and I got out, approached the car, introduced myself to the driver, and told him to drive ahead of me to the Police Station. He agreed, but at the first opportunity, he drove off at high speed. I found out that he was staying in a probation hostel at the end of a prison sentence, so he was in breach of probation and could be arrested. I went to the hostel and in the face of much hostility from the residents arrested the driver. The residents promised me that I wouldn't get a conviction because they would all be witnesses against me.

I took the driver in and found that he was also subject to a suspended sentence, which this offence could bring into being. The case ended up in Crown Court. I didn't call the little girl, she was too young, so I had no witnesses. I gave my evidence and then the driver denied driving. Four of his friends gave evidence, all denying that he was driving and claiming that it was one of them, attributing my evidence to corrupt vindictiveness. My version against five people giving a consistently different version, I could well be in trouble here. The Judge gave a summing up clearly in my favour and I was very relieved when a verdict of guilty was returned. In the sentencing, the Judge sent him to prison and told him the sentence had been increased for his attack on the honour and integrity of a Police Officer. Those were the days!

Police Officers do have discretion about what action to take and I liked to use that discretion, believing that a good telling off could often be just as effective as taking someone to court, and by so doing generate good will towards the police. The ones I tended to take action against were people who were rude and argumentative. The only trouble with that policy was that a high proportion of the people I reported pleaded not guilty. That meant that I had to attend court more often than most. I used to be quite indignant with people who denied committing the offence I had seen, but I came to realise that often, particularly in a motoring offence they really believed that they hadn't gone through a red light, or overtaken within the area of a pelican crossing or failed to stop on demand etc. The conflicting accounts of witnesses could be quite remarkable; it was sometimes difficult to believe that they had seen the same thing. Despite the frequency of my court appearances, I never lost a single case in all my service, which is a record I was very pleased with. It was a close run thing sometimes but I used what I had learned from Sgt Frank on many an occasion when I thought I was in trouble, and as the disqualified driver incident demonstrated, I must have an honest face!

Chapter 14 Courage

Police Officers inevitably face dangerous and potentially dangerous situations on a regular basis and need to find enough courage to face these situations and deal with them. Almost every day there are incidents which require courage, most of them lead to nothing, but it is impossible to know that at the time. On every occasion when an Officer faces an angry man, or a crowd, or a drunk, there is danger. We are not supermen and a blow in the face or a kick in the groin can be incapacitating.

I was called to a noisy party one night. We attended many such calls. Most of them were little problem and people were co-operative. However, with the presence of alcohol, and the increasing use of drugs, there was always the danger that people would act out of character and become aggressive and violent. I had attended my share of those, on one occasion when there was an aggressive reaction to my presence, I was dealing with that, and while I was, other partygoers came out of the back of the house, went round to the front and damaged my police car. On another call, there was a very antagonistic man who slammed a door in my face in an attempt to provoke trouble. On yet another visit a fight was going on between two men over a girl. In separating them, their friends took umbrage and there was real danger of them all having a go at me. Fortunately, I managed to calm them down and order was restored.

As I approached this particular party, it was really noisy. I eventually made myself heard at the door which was answered by a giant of a man, around 6` 6" I would think. Behind him were a number of men of similar size, they turned out to be a rugby team celebrating the day's victory. They were very boisterous and by the look of it, very drunk. I gulped and trying to sound confident and assertive, told him they were making too much noise and I wanted them to turn down the volume. 'OK officer, we don't want any trouble with you.' 'I don't want any trouble with you either,' I replied with heartfelt sincerity! Courage is nothing to do with size or ability but is rather a state of mind. True courage is shown by those who experience fear but are able to overcome it, rather than those who are daft enough to feel no fear.

I related the story earlier of a big strong Sergeant who had no bottle and avoided his responsibility and duty to attend and deal with a violent situation. I would like to say that I possessed enormous courage and faced every situation with fearless wisdom, but it would not be true. I found that I could cope with some things better than others, and it was important to know one's strengths and weaknesses.

Being humble, I will start this chapter with a failing. I don't like heights; in fact, they scare me to death, so when there was a call to a potential suicide from a high building my heart sank. I went to one such call and approached the person on a balcony. I got close enough to talk to him, I tried to persuade him to come down, and I knew that a brave man would seek to distract him and then grab him but I just could not do it. Another colleague who had no such failings joined me. As I talked to the man, my colleague moved with great speed, grabbed the man and pulled him back to safety. I suspect I would have let him jump rather than be able to do what my colleague did. On another occasion, a man was threatening to jump from the river bridge. It's not very high really, but high enough to be difficult for me. The man had climbed over the bridge and was balanced precariously on a narrow parapet. As I talked to him and tried to summon up the courage to grab him, the same colleague leapt over the bridge on to the parapet, grabbed the man and hauled him back to safety, in one swift movement. By the time I had summoned up enough courage he could have jumped.

On the positive side, I was out on mobile patrol one day and picked up a foot patrol to give him a little ride round. A call came in that following a serious domestic dispute a man had driven off in his BMW with the expressed intention of killing himself by crashing into someone else. Due to his state of mind, there was real concern that he would carry out this threat. We sped up to the area and commenced searching for him. We quickly picked him up, driving at high speed through a housing estate. I gave chase as he drove much to fast, past mothers with their children, old people out for their shopping etc.

After a few minutes, he made the mistake of driving down a cul-de-sac. Realising his mistake he spun round at the bottom and drove back towards me. Parked cars narrowed the road so that it would be very difficult to pass each other. I put on my headlights, two-tone horns and blue light, positioned myself in the middle of the road and drove straight at him. In that brief moment I realised that here was an opportunity to stop him, which may not come again, and if he really wanted to hit someone I was going to give him his chance. There was a kind of strangled cry of alarm and fear from the PC in the back seat as I continued to accelerate straight at the BMW! At the last moment, the BMW swerved and crashed into the parked cars. We arrested him and took him in for assessment under the Mental Health Act. My passenger decided I was completely mad and for some reason said that he never wanted to go out with me again! I know that If the BMW hadn't swerved I would have not have swerved away, I would have hit him. Was I brave or mad? Not quite sure really!

I'm particularly ashamed of this incident, but in the interest of truth, I will relate it. I was on early shift on a cold winter's day with snow and ice on the road making travel hazardous. There were a number of accidents and I attended one on a main road leading out of the town. A motorcyclist had skidded on the ice to avoid a car and come off his bike and was lying in the road. The car driver was uninjured but the motorcyclist clearly had a badly broken leg. I called for an ambulance and told them to warn the crew of how slippery the road was. All I could do then was gently move the man to the side of the road and try to reassure him and keep him warm and comfortable as we waited. It wasn't long before we heard the sirens and an ambulance hove into sight. I was a little concerned at the speed he was travelling in the circumstances. The driver saw us on the other side of the road to him, turned his wheel, and braked. The ambulance went into a slide and came straight towards us! I only had little more than a second to react, instinct took over and I leapt out of the way. Unfortunately, the injured motorcyclist couldn't move and a tragic accident looked inevitable. The motorcyclist was close to the edge of the road by a grass bank. The ambulance crashed into the bank and stopped with its front quivering over the terrified motorcyclist and its wheels inches from his head. The impact with the bank had brought the ambulance to a stop in the nick of time! I'd like to say that I knew that would happen, but it would not be true.

When the ambulance crew had recovered a little, the poor motorcyclists leg was splinted, he was put on a stretcher and taken off to hospital. I wasn't sure what he would need treatment for first, a broken leg or shock! I wished I had reacted better and tried to save him, although it is possible that by doing so we would both have been hit. So often, there are only seconds or less to make decisions and instinct can very easily take over from reason, that's my excuse anyway!

One busy night duty I was called to a nightclub in the town centre where there was a report of trouble. I was on my own at the time. I responded to the call and found a group of men at the door doing a lot of shouting and threatening. I managed to calm things down enough to determine what was going on. It seemed that there had been trouble inside the club and the bouncers had decided to eject a customer. This man was big and strong and they had been unable to overcome him and throw him out. Both bouncers had facial damage from the altercation. The manager saw what was happening and came to their aid, armed with a billhook. If you don't know what that is, it comprises a wooden handle and rising vertically from the centre of the handle is a large, strong metal hook, the primary use of this tool is for moving large bales of hay. The manager had hit the man over the head with this weapon and while he was stunned, they had managed to eject him from the club.

He was now on the pavement raging and threatening revenge. The billhook had ripped his scalp open from the front to the back of his head. A terrible injury, which would need some 60 stitches. He was bleeding profusely and was absolutely furious, almost beyond reason. He was indeed a very big man, standing well over six feet tall and built like the side of a house. I tried to calm him but he was raging and determined to exact revenge on the manager, and he moved towards the doorway, which was blocked by the two bouncers. 'Where's that manager, look what he's done to me, I'm gonna rip his fucking head off and shove it up his arse, I'm going to break his arms and stamp on his balls, I'm gonna...' I went and stood between him and the doorway and said to him, 'you are not going back in there.' 'Who's going to stop me?' 'I am.' He looked down at me, and I looked up at him defiantly, I knew I couldn't stop him and he knew it as well. I could almost see his mind working furiously and I held my breath. After what seemed an age he laughed, 'you've got bottle, I'll give you that.' With a sigh of relief, I knew the danger had passed. I persuaded him to come with me to the hospital for treatment and we had a good chat on the way and got on fine. The bouncers didn't want to complain about him and he refused to make a complaint against the manager. I'm fairly confident that he would look to get his own back at some time in the future, well away from any nosey Policeman.

There were many incidents like that, where for a moment things hung in the balance. We would be attacked or they would listen to reason, there was no way of knowing. Unfortunately, people often aren't reasonable, especially when fuelled by drink or drugs, or desperate not to lose face in front of their peers. I always tried to talk my way out of a situation, I don't think I ever struck first, and my face bears testimony to that, my nose used to be straight! Maybe it was pride, believing that my silver tongue could win the day, or was it courage?

So was I brave man or a cowardly man or just confused? I suggest most of us are like me, we have strengths and weaknesses. Thankfully, I was part of a team, others can often cover our weaknesses, and our strengths can be used to help others so that together we might achieve what the organisation needs. Working together, we were able to encourage each other and face situations as required. Often I would find a burst of adrenaline, which came into play when I really needed it, heightening all my senses and abilities. For example chasing after a suspect provided motivation which overcame tiredness and shortage of breath as all the focus was on catching the so and so. When need dictated that I drove very fast, my abilities, such as they were, seemed to be sharper and my reactions faster. Nevertheless, there were things I always found so difficult. I would have liked to be able to overcome my weaknesses and be brave in every circumstance, but it was beyond me and I guess no one is perfect in the real world.

One or two men who I thought of as among my toughest and bravest colleagues shocked me by standing back when confronted by odds that they didn't like. I lost a lot of respect for them, because I saw that these men, who had seemed so fearless, were in fact little more than cowards when they didn't relish the odds. They tried to portray their decision not to pursue the confrontation as wisdom, but I knew that it was in fact fear. How different they were if the odds were in their favour. I suppose the police has always attracted its share of bullies. Others who seemed so quiet and unassuming, showed the hearts of lions when push came to shove. They usually weren't the biggest or the toughest, they never sought confrontation, but they were prepared to put themselves on the line where necessary, whatever the odds. Such men are the backbone of the police and a fine example to younger officers.

Chapter 15 Playing away

Inevitably, most of our time was spent working in the area where we were stationed, but there were occasions when we were deployed elsewhere because of a particular local need there. I hadn't been a Policeman for very long before there was a miners strike. It was nothing like the strike of 1984 but we were formed into what they at that time called mobile columns, and sent off to supplement the local police at various pits in the north of England. We were never actually deployed on the picket lines and the strike petered out. The good thing about the trip was that I acquired a pair of handcuffs. At that time, we were not issued with handcuffs and had to buy some if we wanted them. As we prepared to make our way north we were all issued with new handcuffs still in their boxes. On our return, we had to hand back our handcuffs and they were all checked in. I did hand in my box, but there were no handcuffs in them, they remained with me for the rest of my service!

In the mid 1970's there was a large pop festival at a seaside resort on the north Larkshire coast. Police Officers were drawn from all over the county to police the event. We were billeted in army barracks in a large town nearby, and deployed each day, working at least 12 hour shifts and some times as much as 16 hours. The festival goers put together a tented village to live in while they enjoyed the event, which took place over an Easter weekend. Many of the festival goers were anti-police and there were a high number of drug users so there was a steady stream of arrests and confrontations. Petty crime was a problem all round the area. Dealing with it was difficult, we did go on the site if really necessary, but were very aware that a little spark could flare into an ugly confrontation. If we could catch offenders off the site that was fine, but we had to leave it at that.

The most interesting duty was to keep an eye on the tented village. There was a good chance of finding drugs on people coming on and off the site, and those going on were worth a check for some of the property stolen round the area. Our actions made relationships tense, but the tension never developed further. On the site, tents of all shapes and sizes had sprung up, together with makeshift shelters of blankets, towels and anything they could find. There were no mobile toilets so an area at the back of the camp was used and men and women blithely urinated and defecated in full view of everyone. They were also into 'free love' and it was not unusual to see naked couples copulating in full view of everyone, why they didn't go into their tents is beyond me, true exhibitionism! We took no action, it was flouting public decency but taking action risked a major confrontation, there were only police to see it, and we were certainly not offended, in fact most of us enjoyed the show. There were very occasional passing pedestrians who hurried by, eyes averted, but they never complained.

On one occasion, there was a couple heavily into intercourse with the man thrusting away and the woman's legs wrapped round his waist. The other village occupants acted as if this was a perfectly normal part of their experience and continued on their own business, but then a tent flap opened near the couple and a naked man emerged. As he saw them, a certain part of his anatomy went very quickly from rest to alert! It is very difficult for a naked man to feign disinterest and we were grateful for a good laugh. The things we poor Policemen had to put up with! As three of us were watching such events - all in the course of duty you understand - a young woman came along with a child. She stopped to see what we were looking at and we tried to shield her from such sights and got chatting. She was a single mother and clearly hoped to attract a man. We all behaved impeccably and declined her invitation to go back to her house with her. Perhaps there really is something attractive about men in uniform, or was she just desperate.

When we were off duty, army chefs fed us very well and then there was the bar. At the end of our four days there, I was told that we had drunk an average of eight pints per man per day! Can't be right can it? We could certainly afford it as most of us were working rest days, being paid time and a half for 12 hours per day and double time for the two bank holidays.

Police pay was still very poor at this time, but then Margaret Thatcher came to power. Over the next couple of years, our pay went up around 30% and was tied to a formula, which ensured regular sensible increases without argument. No wonder so many Policemen loved Maggie!

In North Larkshire, there were a number of industrial sites, an oil refinery and a power Station among them. From time to time, a major industrial dispute would break out and the local police needed help. We were sent over to help them. We were told that there were mass pickets outside the power Station and the mood was ugly. Our job was to try to keep the peace, to facilitate entry and egress for those who wanted to cross the picket line and to deal with any troublemakers. We were bussed to the scene and found things very much as we had been briefed. We deployed round the entrance, an all too thin blue line facing the mass pickets. When a vehicle tried to go in or out the pickets would surge forward, we would try to hold them back while a small deputation was allowed to approach the driver and try to persuade him not to continue with his course of action. Most of them did want to continue and we then had to force back the crowd, amidst attempts to stop the vehicle while insults and some missiles were hurled.

In the eyes of the pickets, we soon became the enemy and tension rose. We had no form of protection if things turned ugly, and were expected to form a line holding the back of the belt of the men either side of us. That gave the line a certain strength but it left our front completely unprotected, and no hands to defend ourselves. Police officers are trained and operate as individuals and turning us into a disciplined force was not easy. Inevitably, some officers couldn't stand the insults and missiles that came their way. They broke ranks and plunged into the crowd of pickets seeking their quarry. Some of them got into difficulty and needed to be rescued, and their absence weakened the line and made us all more vulnerable.

The senior officer told us that we were to ignore verbal abuse and only effect an arrest if really necessary, the direction was obeyed and we just had to grin and bear it as an uneasy peace descended. That was until a mini van came from inside the plant and approached the entrance. Pickets moved forward to stop it and talk to the driver. The mini van did not stop, so one of the pickets stood in front of it, that made no difference and the van continued, sweeping up the picket on his bonnet and eventually depositing him in a heap on the road some 30 feet further on. Thankfully, he wasn't seriously hurt. As we struggled to hold back the incensed pickets, a police officer broke ranks, ran across to the van driver and in full view of everyone vigorously pumped his hand in congratulations!

This PC's astonishing actions did wonders for our relationship with the pickets! Senior Officers and the local PC were furious. As the local PC pointed out, when we all went back to our Stations, he would be left trying to retain his relationship with the local people, a relationship which was seriously damaged by that kind of idiotic behaviour.

As well as industrial disputes, there was an occasional need for extra officers at big sporting events such as Rovers Football Club when they were playing a major team. Most of the local police regularly did football duty and were able to help us rare interlopers. We were also sent down to the coast sometimes during the summer months to help police the holidaymakers, many of them day-trippers from some of the big towns whose idea of a good day out was to get legless in the local pubs. We had to pull the odd one out of the harbour, throw them out of pubs and shops, protect women and prevent any crime and public order problems. Only as a very last resort, did we make arrests, not only did they take us off the street, they also risked having to return to give evidence in a subsequent court case.

On the whole, we welcomed these breaks from routine, they often involved considerable extra hours and thus extra pay, most of us enjoyed the comradeship of being together so much, and used the opportunity to broaden our experience and meet others from a variety of places, as well as having a good drink and honing our card playing skills. We often marvelled at the decisions of some of our senior officers and enjoyed a good grumble, although for the most part we probably couldn't have done much better!

Chapter 16 Sexual Crimes

Sadly, there are always a number of sexual offences being committed from indecent exposure to rape and incest. Where possible woman police officers together with CID dealt with them, but often uniform officers had to respond to the initial call.

One of the first sexual offences that I had to deal with was one sunny morning when I was on mobile patrol. I parked the car by a small park and walked round enjoying the sunshine. In the middle of the park was a public convenience and I looked in as I went by. In the gents, one of the cubicles was locked and the noise emanating from it certainly didn't sound like someone relieving themselves! I listened for a while and then went into the next cubicle and looked over the top to see two men engaging in an act of gross indecency. I have to admit that I was angry and disgusted. Standing outside the cubicle, I shouted at them to come out, and to come out now. Two shamefaced men emerged rearranging their clothes. I questioned them to find that they were both married men in their thirties, one of them with children. They had never met before, but had come to the convenience in the hope of just such a meeting. I told them that they had committed an arrestable offence and if I took them in, they would have to bear the disgrace and shame they would bring on their families, the press would inevitably get hold of the story, and the implications for their employment were grim. They both pleaded with me not to take them in, promising not to repeat the offence and painting a desperate picture of the effect on their families of a court appearance. Public perception of such offences were very much more traditional in those days and the picture we had painted between us was very real.

I didn't want to destroy their lives and as it happened, I was the only person to be offended, and I most certainly was. If members of the public had been there, I certainly would have arrested them. In the end, I threatened them with dire consequences if they ever did repeat the offence and ended by saying, 'now get out of my sight both of you, you disgust me.' I did check public conveniences more regularly from then on but I never saw them again, and I never want to.

A mother rang to say that her young daughter had been indecently exposed to. I went to the house and with the mother, tried to get the story from the little girl who was approximately seven years old. After a little prompting we got the story from her, she was walking across a bridge near her home when a man stood in front of her and performed the classic opening of a long coat to reveal a part of himself a little girl certainly didn't want to see. I gently asked her if she remembered what the man looked like. The little girl replied tearfully, 'Big and red with veins all over.' She couldn't give me a description of the man but she certainly remembered something else! We searched the area but without a description, we had little chance of finding the man.

I had about four years service when I attended another call about an indecent exposure. This time the girl was about 10 years old, walking home from school when a man came out of an alley and exposed himself to her. She was able to give a reasonable description of the man, remembering clothing, hair colour, height, build and was able to give an estimate of age. I wanted to determine how accurate her description was so I asked her how tall she thought I was and her estimate was quite close. I then went on to ask her how old she thought I was. At the time I was 26, she estimated 42! That really cheered me up and I determined not to use that method of determining the accuracy of people's descriptions in future! My colleague thought it was very funny, but I wasn't sure that I could see the joke.

As in every town, there was some prostitution, but unless it was pretty blatant, I, in common with the majority of male officers, tended to overlook it, even when I was offered a freebie! As a young PC, I was on patrol with a much more senior PC when we got talking to a lady of doubtful virtue. We were advising her about her behaviour, and she feared arrest, to avoid that she offered us a freebie. I of course said no thank you, but my colleague gratefully accepted! He went with her to her nearby flat and emerged about 20 minutes later, looking rather flushed and red in the face. We knew nothing of aids in those days, but

I asked him if he was concerned about other sexually transmitted diseases. He assured me that he wasn't because he'd been in the services and had already caught most of them!

Unlike male officers, female officers were very hot on prostitution, which they seemed to view as a personal insult. I also found that in allegations of rape or other serious sexual assault, we men were more likely to believe the story of a distressed female than some of the women officers. Perhaps we were more gullible, too easily responding to a woman's tears, or the female officers were bringing their greater experience in such matters to bear.

For the first few years of my service, I lived with my wife and young family in a flat near the River Downs. We became friendly with our neighbours, especially the couple directly opposite to us. They decided it was time to move on and put their flat up for sale. Among the viewers, a man turned up without an appointment and was allowed in by the woman of the flat. Once inside he exposed himself to her and indecently assaulted her. He fled when she screamed, and sadly I wasn't at home at the time. The offence was logged and passed to the WPC's unit for action. They had a heavy caseload and the chances of an arrest were not very good. I wasn't having crimes like that so close to home so I resolved to track down the offender.

I obtained a good description and went round knocking on neighbours doors in the vicinity, and asked in the local pub without much success. I reasoned that there was a good chance that the offender had a record of previous crimes, so I went through all the known sexual offenders and picked out four of them who fitted the description. I then set out to determine where they were at the time and was able to eliminate two of them; one in prison and one moved away. Then I went to see the other two. The first man had an alibi so I moved on to the second man. As soon as I started talking to him, it was pretty obvious to me that here was the guilty party. I arrested him and took him to the Station where I explained the arrest to the Station Sergeant and put the offender in the charge room. I left him there for a few minutes and then returned with a very large pair of scissors. 'You know what I'm going to do with these,' I said menacingly as I advanced on him. His reaction was to cower in the corner and begin crying. My anger melted away and I couldn't help feeling sorry for this inadequate man. He readily admitted the offence and was duly charged and taken to court where he pleaded guilty and was given a suspended sentence and probation. The little incident with the scissors wasn't mentioned, another breach of the rules, but I didn't do it to extract a confession, he did do it, he didn't confess falsely and he was never arrested again during my time at Brightstone.

The most common offence of a sexual nature was indecent phone calls. It was very difficult to do much about it unless a pattern emerged with the same woman getting a series of calls. The best advice we could give was to keep a whistle by the phone and give such a caller a real blast; they didn't usually come back for more! Of course, the fear was that the calls were the precursor to some sort of attack, but that was exceedingly rare. Some women who received these calls were well educated in things of a sexual nature and coped competently, seemingly more amused than shocked. Some other women were very inexperienced in such matters and were thus much more vulnerable. I recall one woman who rang to report such a call. The conversation went something like this, 'I've had a phone call and I think it was one of those indecent calls.' 'What made you think it was indecent?' 'Well he asked me if I was wearing stockings and suspenders and what colour knickers I had on.' 'Well, that certainly sounds like an indecent call, what else did he say?' 'He asked me what I wear in bed and then he got all kind of breathless and said he was having a wink. What is a wink?' 'I think you'd better ask your husband about that madam!'

A new phenomenon arose with the advent of streaking, which most people laughed at or dismissed as foolish and inconsequential, but could upset and shock some people. We had a call one night about a naked man running round an estate and knocking on people's windows, some of whom were very frightened. We had a look round and found the young man responsible, still running round naked. He had been at a party, had too much to drink and been dared to streak round the block. He sobered up pretty quickly when we got hold of him! We gave him a stern talking to and then made him walk in front of us, still naked, back to the party while we followed, illuminating him for all to see with our headlights! I don't think he will do it again!

Inevitably, there were many other sexual offences that I have not mentioned, particularly perhaps incest and sexual abuse of children.

Occasionally uniformed officers attended the initial call, although this was far from ideal, a plain-clothes officer would visit if at all possible. Abuse from someone outside of the family circle was one thing, abuse within the immediate family was quite another. Sadly, the children involved often felt guilty themselves, although they had done nothing wrong. Regrettably, some of the children were damaged for life. These matters were so difficult to deal with, if the father was the offender the child usually didn't want her dad locked up, she just wanted it to stop. The mother could find it very difficult to believe, and other members of the family could turn against the child for causing so much trouble. The WPC's unit dealt with these matters sensibly and sensitively, in liaison with Social Services. I encountered one or two children who had been abused, and so feared the possible consequences that they would not report what had been happening to them.

Sexual harassment in the workplace was almost unheard of in my day, and women dealt with most problems themselves. It did occasionally rear its ugly head in police circles. The action taken was a reprimand and perhaps a transfer. The offence would have to be serious for court action to be contemplated, and of course, this was a long time before industrial tribunals, and the litigious nature of our present society. Methods of dealing with such matters tended to be more practical; in one incident I particularly remember, a PC tried to grope a civilian woman driver and she hit him over the head with a telephone, one of the old heavy ones. A very effective deterrent!

It seems to be the case that a large number of sexual crimes are never reported to the police. There are a variety of reasons for that, including trepidation about the police and the process, of examinations by doctors, cross-examination in court and of course retribution from the offender or his associates. More than once I was called to see a member of a family, usually the mother, who feared something had happened to her daughter. After a lot of persuasion, the daughter told me that she had been raped, in one case by a stranger and in the second case by an uncle. Try as I might I could not persuade either girl to make a complaint. The offenders walked free, free to do it again, and there was absolutely nothing we could do about it.

A positive step in the area of most sexual offences, especially those involving children, is to continue to work towards a police service, which is accessible and caring, active in schools, youth clubs and the community generally. Time spent on such activities may not be reflected in the statistics so important in police circles these days. However, although the results are not quantifiable, reason indicates that there will be long term benefits, not only in an increased willingness to report sexual offences, but also in goodwill towards the police. There were such schemes in my day and I understand they have now been further extended, through Community Relations Officers and the like. Long may it continue.

Chapter 17 The Promotion Game

When I joined the police, I had high hopes of becoming a Chief Constable or at least a rank close to that, and the first hurdle was to pass the promotion exams. Accordingly, I made myself settle down to hard study. I bought an expensive correspondence course and worked hard for almost a year. The exam consisted of two papers, Traffic law and then Crime and General Duties, I believe they were called. The exam was conducted under strict conditions. The scope of law is so wide it is almost impossible to know everything thoroughly, so there had to be reasoned deductions over the likely subjects, and the hope that the questions would cover the area where knowledge was strongest. I'm glad to say that I managed to pass the Sergeants Exam at the first attempt. For my efforts, I was awarded the princely sum of £45, only a small fraction of the cost of a correspondence course, and was now eligible to apply for a promotion board. At this stage, I had only about three years service, I did apply for a promotion board but was not surprised to be turned down.

Undaunted I continued with my studies to sit the Inspectors Exam. This time I bought a memory-training course and worked on that, it was a great help, especially in remembering acts, sections and stated cases. The only trouble is that I've forgotten it now! I sat the exam the following year and to my great delight passed with flying colours, especially as I got another £45! I was now qualified for promotion to the rank of Inspector. However, promotion was not automatic, as it was in the Metropolitan Police. In Larkshire candidates had to be recommended locally and pass an interview before a specially constituted Force Selection Board. Competition was fierce, and some men would do everything they could to promote their cause, agreeing with their Senior Officers at every turn, even when they were talking gibberish, and generally 'kissing butt' as our American cousins would put it. I wasn't going to do that. I still had a, probably misguided, faith that those in positions of authority would see through such behaviour.

The police also have an accelerated promotion system. Applicants for the force who have a degree can apply to join the police through this accelerated promotion scheme and undertake a series of interviews and tests, before they join. If successful, they start the job as a Constable, stay in that rank for two years, which must be satisfactory, and they must take and pass the Sergeants Exam at the first attempt. They then go to Bramshill Police College for one year of study. If that is satisfactory, they are promoted to Sergeant, and are required to perform one year of satisfactory service in that rank. Automatic promotion to Inspector follows, with every expectation of reaching the very highest levels of the service.

There was provision for officers who had joined in the normal way to apply for accelerated promotion after two years satisfactory service and a first time pass of the Sergeants Exam. A degree clearly helped but was not obligatory. I decided to have a go at that and put in an application. The first hurdle was to be recommended at divisional level and I negotiated that hurdle successfully. It was then on to a Force wide selection process and here my application came to an end, it was worth a go I suppose.

About this time, I was seconded to Headquarters to join a small team of officers set up to undertake the computerisation of personnel records. I didn't want to go, but I had no choice, at least it would be 9-5 with weekends off which would be a pleasant change. Larkshire Police now had access to the computer at a nearby town, which was maintained by the Larkshire County Council. I went over to look at it and was taken into a very large room, absolutely full of computer hardware, all tapes whirring and lights flashing. They were so proud of this futuristic computer, and I was duly impressed. It's strange to think that my current Laptop has more memory and power than all the equipment in that room! My colleagues for this task were a nice bunch of very senior PC's, all having upward of 20 years service. We were under the direction of a Superintendent and he was responsible to an Assistant Chief Constable. I realised that a useful feature of this secondment could be that I had regular contact with senior officers at HQ, useful in the sense that when and if I got on a promotion board I would face men who knew me personally. That should be helpful, shouldn't it, as long as I made the right impression?

The work itself was fairly routine and repetitive, but the quicker we got it done, the quicker I could go back to real police work. Fortunately, I got on very well with my colleagues, which made things much easier. The intention was that when all the records were computerised the Personnel Department could be slimmed down, as their workload would be significantly reduced. Perhaps you won't be surprised to hear that the outcome was rather different. We finished the task after around five months, during which time senior officers began to appreciate the statistics they could obtain from a computer. The upshot of this discovery was that the Personnel Department, instead of being reduced, employed an extra person to focus on extracting statistics from the computer and liasing with computer staff. What did we do before computers?

I often ate in the HQ dining room, and was even occasionally allowed in the wood panelled, hallowed hall of the Senior Officers Dining Room, but only by special invitation. I also made occasional visits to the HQ bar. In that way I got to know many of the HQ staff of various ranks. On route to giving up smoking, I had left cigarettes behind and moved on to cigars. A Chief Inspector approached me one day and asked for a cigar as he had run out. Being a generous sort of chap, I gave him a cigar. Unsolicited he promised to return the favour in the near future. A few days later, I was in HQ Bar in a group, which included this Chief Inspector. He produced a packet of large cigars in a cigar case, the sort of size cigars that Churchill would have been proud of. He then said he would like to give me one of his if I wanted one. I said that was good of him and accepted, whereupon he tipped the case up and holding the large cigars back extracted a tiny manikin, which he gave me. Observing this some of my colleagues expressed the view that he was confirming his reputation as being as tight as a certain part of the anatomy of a duck!

On the same day and quite near us in the bar were the Chief Constable and other very senior staff. Choosing his moment carefully this Chief Inspector observed this entire group getting fresh drinks and then stepped forward. 'Can I buy you a drink, sir?' he said to the Chief Constable. 'We've all just got one thank you, but seeing as it's you we'll all have one.' With that he turned to all those around him and said, 'come on boys, Jim is buying a drink!' Poor old Chief Inspector Jim, trying hard to look happy about it, was forced to buy a big round. The observant Chief Constable went up in my estimation!

Our work at HQ took us through Christmas, which meant that we would have Christmas and Boxing Day off, a real treat. On Christmas Eve, the staff started leaving around midday and by 1500 HQ was like a ghost town. The Superintendent in charge came to see us and explained that he couldn't let us go without the ACC's permission and he daren't ask the ACC because he was in a terrible mood having lost his cat! The workings of the corridors of power in all their glory.

The work at HQ completed, I returned to Brightstone and back on section. There was a new, and very good, crew in the emergency vehicle now. It wouldn't have been right to try to take over from them so I found myself doing some months on Station Officer duties, training new recruits, occasionally helping out in the clerk's office and finding some time for patrol duties.

The Station office could be a very busy environment. With a telephonist, the Station Officer had to try to deal with phone, local radio, force radio and personal callers. Calls and incidents were recorded in the 'Occurrence Book' or OB. This was a bound volume, which had to be kept in pristine condition, every entry neatly entered in fountain pen to the satisfaction of senior officers, especially the Chief Superintendent. He would make at least a weekly visit and always found something wrong, bless him. No abbreviations were allowed and I well remember his indignation when he found someone had written about an accident involving an articulated vehicle and described it as an R√

I enjoyed the time in the Station office as long as I could go out from time to time. More than once, I couldn't resist running out of the Station to join officers dealing with trouble at a local pub, or some other local incident. Out of office hours, the Station Officer was also responsible for caring for prisoners in the cells, who always seemed to want something. Excitement was limited but being so busy was fulfilling in its own way. Thus time passed with its usual quota of adventures, some of which I have described, together with times of routine.

By now I had nearly five years service, a real old hand! I was sent on a five-year refresher course, another four weeks at Headquarters. More struggling to keep awake, I don't think classrooms agree with me. It was useful in brushing up on the law and fitness. Some of the instructors were interesting characters. There was an Inspector responsible for teaching us our civil defence responsibilities. The cold war was still in full flow and he was certain that there would be nuclear war. In preparation, he had installed an underground shelter in his back garden. Its steel structure was so big and heavy that it had to be delivered by helicopter. Then he worried that all the neighbours would know of its existence and try to muscle in, so he armed himself with a shotgun in readiness!

This same Inspector took us for some sessions on firearms. All confiscated weapons came to him. Most were disposed of but interesting ones were retained for training purposes. He came into possession of an industrial nail gun, complete with ammunition. The cartridges were of varying strengths. He chose the highest strength ammunition, went outside to the perimeter fence and fired the nail gun into a 4" concrete post. To his horror, he looked at the hole to see that the nail had gone straight through and out across the fields where a number of women were busy picking strawberries! Thankfully, he didn't hit anyone.

The next time we were with him he was amusing himself by waiting until he thought we looked soporific and then discharging a firearm, loaded with blanks. It was a deafening noise in the confines of a classroom. The instructor in the next classroom wondered what on earth was going on, and the two instructors were soon engaging in some banter. They were both leaning out of their respective windows, addressing remarks and rude signs to each other. Of course, it wasn't long before a sign appeared saying 'Bang'. Our Inspector leant out of the window and as his brother instructor leant out of his window to continue the fun he fired a gun right alongside his ear. We all laughed but I suspect his colleague was deafened and might had suffered long-term damage. As I said, an interesting character, our Inspector!

The course over I returned to Brightstone and applied again for the promotion board and for the Police College at Bramshill. This time I was accepted to appear before the Force Promotion Board and dates were set. When I looked at the officers on the board, who should be chairing it but the ACC that I had worked for during my attachment to HQ!

With some trepidation, I presented myself at the designated time and sat in front of the three-man board to begin the ordeal. I hate questions like, 'why should we promote you?' 'What do you have to offer that other men don't?' They were inevitably asked and I answered as best I could, trying to balance humility with confidence. Everything seemed to be going pretty well until the ACC said to me, 'the traffic in Brightstone is awful, why haven't you officers at the local Station sorted it out?' I explained that we did our best but ultimately you can't fit a quart into a pint pot and there was simply too much traffic for the existing road network. He persisted with this line of questioning saying how difficult it was for him to get into work because of the traffic. I reiterated my explanation and then concluded, 'If it's such a problem for you sir, the only thing I can suggest is that you do what I have done and buy a moped.' The other two members of the board thought that was hilarious but the ACC certainly didn't, spluttering something about, 'ridiculous, can you see me on a moped!' Had I blown it?

After anxiously waiting for a few weeks, the results were published and I had passed. I was delighted and quite happy to wait until an appointment was made. Back at the Station, whenever there was a shortage of Sergeants I was allowed to have a few days as acting Sergeant. I thoroughly enjoyed the acting Sergeant role, of course, I made a few mistakes, and looking back, I asked the impossible sometimes. However, I was learning and was accepted readily enough by PC's and most of the Sergeants and Inspectors, or at least tolerated. I say most because there was one Sergeant, a very surly ex traffic Sergeant, who would not accept me and tried to make sure that when he was around I had no responsibility. He went so far as to stay on duty until a substantive supervisor came on duty rather than leave me in charge. I was rather fed up with this, disputed with him regularly and looked for an opportunity to show my worth and teach him a little lesson. I know I shouldn't have but I'm only human!

I was on early shift when this Sergeant was on nights. With some difficulty I managed to persuade him to go home and leave me to get on with things, after all there was an Inspector due on duty within the hour. Off he went with a few remarks, leaving me fuming. I saw the early shift out on patrol and did a few administrative tasks in the Sergeants Office. The Inspector came on duty and walked by as I did so. On an impulse, I took the keys for the Sergeants and Inspectors car and dropped them down the back of a filing cabinet, which was situated under the key board. Then I went to see the Inspector and asked him if he had the keys. Clearly he didn't and he asked who last had them, 'Sgt Lark' I replied. 'Well ring him at home and ask him where they are.' By now it was around 0630 and Sergeant Lark should be tucked up in bed. I rang him and you will be surprised to hear that he didn't know where they were and thought he had hung them in their proper place on the board! I waited a while and then at a leisurely pace I went back to the Inspector and told him what had been said and that I couldn't find the keys anywhere.

'Well ring him again and tell him to get his brain in gear and think where they are.' I repeated the process we had just been through with the same result. Returning to the Inspector I told him the bad news and a now angry Inspector said, 'ring him again, tell him to get his arse down here and find those keys!' Concerned for the poor Sergeant I pointed out that he was in bed after nights but the Inspector had no sympathy. Who am I to argue with an Inspector? So I rang Sgt Lark and told him the bad news. By now it was about 0730, one and a half hours after he had gone home. He had no choice but to agree to come in. I reckoned it would take him about 10 minutes to get dressed so I waited 10 minutes and then rang him back, just catching him as he was going out of the door. I told him the good news that I had found the keys down the back of a cabinet under the board. He was relieved and could go back to bed, and me, well I should have felt guilty but I actually felt rather pleased with myself, even if he would never know what really happened.

Not long after I had passed the Force Promotion Board, I heard that I had been successful in my latest application and the Division had recommended me to go forward for selection for accelerated promotion. I had to appear before the Force Selection Board and somewhat to my surprise; I passed that and went on to the next phase, which was an interview at the Home Office in London. At the appointed hour, I duly presented myself at St Anne's Gate in London and appeared before a board made up of five very august gentlemen from various walks of life. Questions were not limited to police matters and ranged over politics and social policies. Britain had only recently joined the EEC and one of them asked for my views on that. Fortunately, I had taken a keen interest in the community and had a reasonable knowledge of it. For the rest of the interview I happily talked with them and answered questions on that subject. About 10 days later, I was called to see the Superintendent who told me that I had been successful. Good old EEC! The final part of the selection process would be a three-day selection conference to be held in a few months time somewhere in the country.

The date and venue eventually came through. The selection was to be held at Preston, Lancashire at the police HQ there. Reaching this stage meant that out of several thousand applicants, I can't remember the exact numbers involved, but there was somewhere in the region of fifty of us left for about two dozen places. I was very nervous as I made the journey to Lancashire. I don't have a degree and didn't even go to grammar school, how would I get on with the best educated of police officers. One of the criteria the selectors would look at was whether applicants had the academic ability to cope with a strenuous and intense year of study. I hoped to use my passes in the promotion exams as an indication of my academic possibilities; I had nothing else to offer. The thought of being watched for three days didn't appeal much either. Anyway I arrived safely enough, was given time to unpack in my room, thankfully we all had individual rooms. We than had to gather together and all the applicants joined together with the selectors, who tried to put us at our ease by asking if we'd had a good journey, wasn't the weather nice, do look for a chance to go into Preston etc. It didn't work! Pleasantries over, we were invited to sit in front of the board. We were introduced to the Selection Board which consisted of a Deputy Chief Constable, the Headmaster of a public school, a naval Admiral, a Chief Superintendent, and I think the others were a Home Office official and a captain of industry. The setting was formal with the board sitting behind a large table. We were immediately asked, addressing us as a group, how we would solve the country's economic ills, and particularly what our views were on the national debt? Clearly, they were looking for natural leaders and those who could think quickly and were well read. I did my best to join in early and say something sensible.

Following that we had an introductory session when we were assured that we wouldn't be watched while we ate to see if we picked up peas on our knife, nor would our conversations outside of sessions be monitored. We were given a timetable and off we went. There were individual interviews with each of the board members, written tests of problem solving and group work where we were given difficult scenarios to negotiate. I think one I had was to convince a council that there was need for a dam on the local river against considerable opposition. The other applicants took the various parts in these exercises and I'm glad to say that most of us didn't destroy each other when we had the chance and tried to be sensitive. I found that I was the oldest applicant at the advanced age of 27. I was the only one without a degree but I was the most experienced as a police officer, if that was going to count for anything.

At the end of a tough and tiring three days, we came to the last exercise. We were told to mark each other and say whether we thought each of us should be approved or rejected. Some of the other applicants were really stressed out about being successful but I was fairly relaxed about it, especially as I had passed a promotion board and knew that I would be promoted in the next few months. I had tried my best throughout the three days and felt that I had given as good an account of myself as I could, and in the last exercise, I came out as the most approved candidate. Then it was farewell and back to Brightstone to await the result.

A few weeks later, I was called in to see the divisional Chief Superintendent to be told that my application had been turned down. Sadly, the reasons were not divulged and remained on the file about us that we never got to see. I was naturally disappointed and knew that there was now little likelihood of my ever being a Chief Constable. However, I had promotion to look forward to and maybe I could advance through the conventional route.

A month or so later my posting came through. I was to be a uniformed Sergeant stationed at Downchester in the group of Downs towns. Sounded pretty good to me, it was only a dozen miles away so we could remain in the house we had by now bought just outside of Brightstone and I could travel, which shouldn't be too bad on shift work. We were called up to HQ to meet with the Chief Constable. He told us of his expectations of us and asked if we were all happy with our posting? Before anyone could answer, he went on, 'because if you are not, I will change it for you, but I will take your stripes!' In the circumstances, no one wanted to change their posting. I went back to my Station and settled down, determined to enjoy my last few weeks at Brightstone before the new adventure started.

Chapter 18 Last few months as a Constable

Those last few months at Brightstone gave me time to think and to try to make sure my experience was as wide as possible. Some of my colleagues seemed to want to help me! The licensing Inspector spoke to me on the first day of a night shift. 'How much service have you got now?' 'Six years, sir.' 'And how many people have you arrested for drinking and driving?' 'Five or six I suppose.' 'Five or six in all that time! I expect to see you bring someone in this set of nights, is that clear?' 'Yes, sir.' I then ignored him and carried on as before. After three nights, he asked me if I had arrested anyone yet. I admitted that I hadn't. 'I order you to bring someone in before the end of this set of nights, is that clear?' 'Yes, sir, I will do my best.' Not sure that was a lawful order, anyway I ignored it. On the last night, he asked me again if I had arrested anyone, I had to admit that I had not. 'Right, I shall come out with you tonight and make sure that you do.' 'That's very good of you sir.' I replied with ill disguised sarcasm! He ignored it.

Soon after 2200, we set out and the hours went by without finding a drunk driver, or even a motoring offence, which would give us the power to stop and request a breath test. 'Not always easy to find one sir, is it?' 'Humph' was the reply. Shortly afterwards we saw a Ford Escort being driven away from the town centre, the car driver was having some difficulty in remaining in the right lane, it looked like an obvious drunk at last! 'After him, you are about to make an arrest for drink driving.' I obediently pursued the car, overtook it and flagged the driver down. As I did so we saw that the driver wasn't a man but a very attractive young woman with long blonde hair. 'I'll deal with this,' cries our gallant Inspector. Leaping out of the car, he went back to the Escort and talked to the young woman. 10 minutes later, he returned to the car, 'okay, we can go now.' 'But what about drink driving?' 'Well she only lives round the corner so I decided that a caution will do!' I looked at him in some amazement, 'did you get her phone number?' 'Of course not, come on, lets go,' he said and so we did. He never mentioned drink driving again!

I often drove a rural area car patrol in those last few months. It was difficult to get a cup of tea anywhere, especially on nights, and it was too far to drive back to the Station. There was one good-hearted farmer who left us a drink in a barn. There was a flagon of cider and four glasses covered by a cloth. Very pleasant it was too and very strong! One was definitely enough. We also found a very rural pub where the licensee was wont to remain open for a select few at the end of licensing hours. I did a surprise visit one night and caught them drinking after time, he bribed me with a pint! From then on, I would call in from time to time for a nocturnal noggin! He was always very discreet and there were no houses nearby to disturb.

I was talking to my colleague, the Licensing Inspector, when he spoke of this pub. He had heard of them drinking after time and was determined to raid the place. I agreed that was a good idea, we couldn't have people doing dreadful things like drinking after time, could we! I offered to accompany him on the raid and he readily agreed. When he called me in to go with him, I slipped away and rang the pub to warn them. The Inspector and three of us then drove out to the pub and gained entry. Do you know, there was no one drinking after hours! We returned to the Station with the frustrated Inspector vowing to catch them next time. Twice more we raided the place, each time I warned them and each time there were no offences! After the third time I suggested to the Inspector that his information must have been wrong and we ought to move on to other things. He reluctantly agreed, and my happy arrangement continued at the pub for a long time. I didn't feel too guilty about it especially after our drink-driving episode!

On one of my last set of nights, I attended a call to the hospital. I found a doctor cornered by a large, aggressive and very drunk woman. She calmed down somewhat and then wanted to kiss the doctor, or rather slobber all over him, and tried to sit on his lap, he didn't seem to keen! I had a colleague with me and we told her that she would have to come with us. 'I've got to have a fucking piss,' she informed us. They didn't want her staggering round the hospital so a nurse wheeled in a commode and she dropped her knickers, sat down in front of us, and noisily deposited a large quantity of steaming urine in the commode! I couldn't help noticing some urine dribbling down her legs as she pulled her knickers up.

We then escorted this charming lady out to our car, I say escort, half carry her and half drag her would be more accurate, and she was no lightweight. We asked her where she lived and took her home. As we went, she treated us to an account of all the troubles in her life, and gave us her views on life in general, spiced with obscenities and self-pity. We were obviously not paying enough attention, and she became agitated. She was sitting behind me in the back seat when she started thrashing about and wrapped her, still wet, legs round my neck. Lovely! We found out that she had broken up with her husband and now lived with her father. We managed to get the address out of her and took her home. Her father took one look at her and said, 'there's no way she's coming in here like that, she's pissed as a newt and she's a right pain when she's like that.' Really!

We called the Station on the radio and told the Sergeant we were bringing in a drunken woman for being drunk and disorderly. 'You're not putting some drunken woman in my nice clean cells to make the place a mess, take her somewhere else!' But where, we wondered? Eventually we got the name and address of a friend and took her there. When we managed to knock her up, her friend was less than pleased to see her, it was now after 0100 and she refused to have her inside her house. Great, what now? We did consider dumping her in the woods, but it was a cold December night and she might not survive the night!

In the end, we took her back to her father's house and almost forced him to take her in, at least for the night. Very relieved, we went back to the Station for a cuppa and for me to wash my neck. We do meet some interesting people! Arresting her would have been more trouble than its worth. Drunks have to be constantly monitored, nine times out of ten they vomit all over the floor and about 50% of the time they wet themselves. The morning shift try to make them clean it up, depending on the state of them. If they can't they have the very unpleasant task to themselves, unless they can persuade a cleaner. If they are taken to court the sentence is minimal so offloading them somewhere is usually the most expedient way of dealing with them.

Sometimes of course, we have no alternative but to make an arrest, especially if the drunk is offering violence. I had to attend the report of a drunk one night, causing trouble at a local pub. When I got there, the man was staggering about outside the pub, shouting curses and threats. We couldn't quieten him down or find out his name and address and he wanted to fight everyone. Reluctantly my colleague and I had to arrest him. We took him back to the Station and got him out of the car. He squared up to us again and we had to manhandle him into the Station, explain to the Station Sergeant why we had brought such a person into his Station and then put him into a cell to sleep it off.

He was ok in the morning and was charged with being drunk and disorderly and taken to court.

He was given a nominal fine and then released. That should have been the end of the matter but he now harboured a grudge against the pub licensee. A week or so later he went back to the pub soon after midnight. He climbed over the rear wall into the yard, intending to cause damage or to steal. Unfortunately for him, the Licensee kept a dog, a rotweiller, which weighed some 12 stones. The dog seized the unfortunate intruder and tore one of his kneecaps out! We attended and called an ambulance to take the stricken man to hospital.

The licensee didn't want to pursue a prosecution, feeling that the man had suffered enough, a sentiment with which I heartily agreed. When the man was patched up and released from hospital some weeks later, he returned to the pub. He was on crutches and crippled for life, but he had returned to apologise for all the trouble he had caused! Thoughts of suing the licensee just didn't arise at that time.

Very early on in my career, and thankfully nothing to do with me, a drunk was brought in and put in the cells. When someone went to visit him, they found him dead, presumably having choked on his own vomit. Drunks should be very frequently checked, I think every 15 minutes was the minimum period between visits. This drunk had only been visited hourly; serious trouble loomed for those involved. They got round it by tearing up the original detention sheet and completing a new one, showing visits every 15 minutes and with a forged signature of the drunk. While this was being done, an ambulance was called and took him off to hospital where he was pronounced dead on arrival. A post mortem examination showed that he had indeed choked on his own vomit. No blame could be attached to the Police because the rules had all been 'complied with.' I certainly learned a lesson from it and I hope all the other officers involved did as well.

Later on in my last set of nights, I was called to trouble at a nightclub on the edge of town. When I got there, the staff told me that there was a man at the bar who was causing trouble, they had tried to chuck him out but he wouldn't go, when they tried to force him, they had lost the argument and he had assaulted staff members causing a few injuries. They warned me that he was a big tough guy. I approached the man and talked to him. He was aggressive and angry and not going anywhere. I told him that either he went quietly or my colleague and I would remove him. Even when he was sitting down I could see that he was a big man. However when he turned and stood up, I found myself staring up at the biggest man I have ever met. He was over seven feet tall with broad shoulders and hands like shovels. If you have seen Richard Kiel in the James Bond movies, this must have been his brother, fortunately without the metal teeth! 'Oh yeah,' he said and stood challenging us to take him on. 'You just think about it while I have a word with the staff and then we will deal with you,' I said, trying to sound confident. We retired out of earshot to formulate a plan. Just then, a Sergeant arrived and joined our discussions.

Plan in place and now ready for the fray we returned to him, 'look, you have to answer for assaulting the staff, I'm sure you don't want to get into any more trouble so we don't want to smash the place up, why don't you just come with us quietly?' 'I'll come outside with you; I'm ready to go home anyway. But if you think you're taking me in, you have another think coming!' We went outside and the Sergeant took the lead and began winding our man up. While his attention was fully focussed down at the Sergeant, who looked so small against this giant, I slipped round behind him and got down on all fours. The Sergeant then rushed forward and pushed him, over me he went, falling full length on the ground. Before he could regain his senses all three of us were on him and he was handcuffed and restrained. The bigger they are the harder they fall! Rather pleased with ourselves we squeezed him into a Transit sized police van, we would never have got him into a normal car, and took him back to the Station where he calmed down and was no further trouble. Good inventive thinking, I'd like to claim it was my idea but it was the Sergeant.

Nights passed and I moved on to day duties. One morning I was in the High Street standing next to my car talking to someone when I heard the unmistakeable sound of a car approaching with a defective exhaust. I turned to look at the car and when I saw the driver, I recognised him immediately and my heart leapt for joy. Out into the road I rushed and stopped him. Do you remember the man I stopped with a senior colleague at 0230 in the morning, recorded in chapter 2, right at the beginning of my career. The rude motorist who refused to answer our questions and challenged us to do anything about it, well it was him! Six years later and I recognised him and he recognised me. What a difference this time, he was respectful, polite and humble.

I looked over his car, checked his documents and looking at his driving licence I found that he hadn't changed his address to the address he had just given me. Another minor offence. 'Give me one good reason why I shouldn't book you?' 'Well, I've learned my lesson, I will never be rude to a police officer again, and I will go and get my exhaust repaired immediately, and send my driving licence straight off.' 'Hmm' I said as I thought about it. I couldn't resist saying, 'will you open your boot please?' And of course, he did without a murmur! Had he learned his lesson? Would I be unnecessarily vindictive if I booked him? I decided I had made him grovel and perhaps clemency was the order of the day, so let him off with a caution. He was very grateful and I hope he had learned his lesson, or had he just had me over? Was I daft or sensibly merciful? I leave it you to decide.

The IRA were very active in England at this time and terrible atrocities had been committed in various places around the country. As a result, there were an inordinate number of hoax calls, and genuine calls about suspicious vehicles and suspect packages. Some officers called for the Army Bomb Disposal Unit on each occasion, and they were under a lot of pressure, with attendance times becoming longer and longer. It was just not practicable to call them out for every incident and so we found that we had to open some of the parcels and packages ourselves. In fact, most people were very happy with that, they only wanted someone else to risk their lives so that they didn't have to! This was not official policy of course; it was simply officers of my level using their common sense. We tried to be as careful as possible and had some training about explosives. There we saw how an ounce or so of explosive could blow a hole right through a block of three-inch thick solid steel! We had a bomb bin at the Station, a circle of lorry tyres, designed to contain the impact of a small bomb and probably completely useless. Inevitably, as the calls continued we got a little blasé and used less care, increasingly believing that the IRA wouldn't come to an insignificant little town like ours, their focus was on the big cities.

A few days before I left Brightstone there was a bomb alert in a pub called the Dog and Duck. Hoax bomb calls to pubs were a regular event around this time. This pub was near the army barracks in Brightstone and was regularly used by army personnel, known universally as squaddies. Nevertheless, like so many calls before this one it was another hoax. I was shortly to go off duty and I sat at the bar over a small glass of cold tea chatting to the Licensee telling him not to worry, as we had no reason to expect an attack in Brightstone. I went back to the Station and thence off duty and thought no more about it.

A few days later, there was another call to the Dog and Duck and a codeword was used. Officers attended and cleared the place and started evacuating nearby houses when the bomb went off. It was in a car, which wrecked the pub and threw the car against a high stone wall opposite the pub. The shock wave of the explosion ricocheted off the wall and across to houses smashing windows for a considerable distance. I was off duty at the time so didn't attend until the next day. I thought about my cavalier attitude and what I had said to the Licensee. Thankfully, no one was killed although there were a number of injuries.

I went to the scene and stood there reflecting. As I stood, looking and thinking, a man approached me. He was elderly and told me that he had been staying in the pub and his life savings were in a tin box under his bed in an upstairs room. The pub was wrecked and was far beyond rebuilding, but the staircase was still intact together with some of the beams supporting parts of the upper floor. Taking pity on the old man I gingerly climbed up the wreckage to the upper floor and found his tin box. I returned covered in dust and glad to be safely down. I gave him the tin, which he opened to reveal that it was stuffed with a wad of notes of various denominations, there must have been several thousands of pounds there. He thumbed through the money and I half thought a fiver or so might be coming my way, but no, he shut the tin, 'thanks officer,' and off he went. I didn't want any of his money anyway and I would have been duty bound to refuse it!

Exhaustive enquiries were immediately made to trace the bombers and they were eventually arrested. It transpired that three or four IRA members had planted the bomb and when they did, they were heavily armed and ready to shoot any unfortunate police officer who tried to stop them. We wouldn't have stood a chance so I'm only glad none of us did. The whole episode was a bit of a shock to many of us and especially to me, who had been so wrong. I understand the terrorists were only caught thanks to some foolish boasting in a pub one night. The whole incident reminded me that you can never tell and need to be vigilant and alert at all times, however unlikely it might seem that an attack would be made in our area. Needless to say, I didn't broadcast my attendance and conversation at the pub a few days before the explosion!

During my time at Brightstone, the vast majority of the residents of the town were white. As time went by some black and Asian people came to live there, and as far as I know, there were no problems at all. Most of them lived among white people rather than congregating together in one area. Only one officer at the Station was black. He had to put up with a certain amount of stick but he took it all in good part. There was no political correctness to worry about and he laughed at things like the night duty Sergeant saying to him, 'and you Henry are walking the High Street beat, and for God's sake keep smiling or no bugger will see you!' We all had to put up with a little bit of stick for various things, and he took no more than anyone else and was a cheerful officer, well liked by his colleagues and good at his job.

Obviously, we did encounter people from other ethnic groups every so often; the most common way was to come into contact with people coming from London or one of the big towns nearby to visit friends and relatives in a local prison. When we had occasion to talk to some of them we often found their attitude very different from the local people.

I saw a car drive through a red light one day and stopped it. Inside were four black men, they were very hostile, accused me of stopping them simply because they were black and called me a 'white honky!' I had never been called that before, and I didn't even know they were black until I stopped them. Trying very hard to remain calm, I told them why I had stopped them and reported the driver for the offence. Perhaps not surprisingly he had no identification on him, and gave me details which I couldn't readily check and I wasn't surprised to find out later were false. They drove off shouting insults and waving v-signs and middle fingers at me as they went. I didn't flourish any v signs but I confess to muttering to myself some abuse, which could have been deemed racist, which I would like to have used in response to theirs. Many of my colleagues had a similar story to tell, most of them had kept their cool, but one or two admitted that they had responded to racist abuse with some of their own.

I realised how difficult it must be for police officers in the big towns and cities to overcome this hatred. They come out of training taught to be non-racist, full of good intentions and very much determined to treat every one equally. Then they found themselves abused and encountered such hostility that it must have been all too easy to be dragged into a them and us culture, thus perpetuating the problems. I am sure these problems can be overcome, but it requires a great deal of self-discipline, tolerance, patience and supervisory support to make any impression.

Those last few months seemed to pass very quickly and it was soon time to leave Brightstone. A none too popular Sergeant had recently left Brightstone, and his departure was rather an unfortunate experience. He put a notice up round the Station inviting people to a farewell drink at HQ bar. Some unkind character took his notices down and replaced them with notices all round the Station saying, 'Sergeant XXX is holding a leaving do in the Telephone Box outside Divisional HQ. All his friends are invited to attend!' The Superintendent went round replacing these notices, but I'm told his farewell drink was not very well attended. With some trepidation I put notices up announcing my farewell drink, (such occasions commonly called PU's!), at HQ bar. As far as I know, my notices weren't tampered with and many of my friends and colleagues came to make sure I was really going! It was great to see a good number there, and it was a lovely evening.

I was 28 years old and had six years and two month's service under my belt. I had thoroughly enjoyed my time, seen a lot and done a lot, and I just hoped that I had learned enough. I left Brightstone and prepared to go on to Downchester with apprehension and excitement about all that might lay ahead, but that's another story!

About the Author

James Cannon (not his real name) lives quietly on the south coast with his wife. He has taken early retirement because of health problems. Retirement has given him the time to write, an ambition for several years. James has two grown up children and is about to become a grandfather for the first time. When he left the police he became a Church of England Vicar until retirement. He intends to write another book about the change from policeman to vicar. James enjoys walking by the sea, reading, writing and time with the family. He takes a keen interest in current affairs, the Church and Police issues. He is a sports fan and supports Brighton and Hove Albion.